MENIERE

AND THE R

MINDFUL RECOVERY

ANSWERS TO HELP YOU FULLY RECOVER FROM MENIERE'S DISEASE

PAGE ADDIE PRESS
UNITED KINGDOM. AUSTRALIA

Copyright

CONTENTS

Preface

Mindful Recovery is the second edition of *The Meniere Answer Book*. I have taken the opportunity in this edition to answer the questions on: How did I make a full recovery from Meniere's disease?

Learn from yesterday,
live for today, hope for tomorrow.
The important thing is not to stop questioning.
- Albert Einstein

INTRODUCTION

Meniere's disease brings with it a lot of questions. And if you are lucky, you might come across a few people who have the same questions, and luckier still, answers.

Answers to questions on how to manage Meniere's disease, with the objective of making a full recovery, are what this book is about.

There is a way out of Meniere's, so I hope, sharing my answers to Meniere's, will help you make a full recovery, just as I have done.

When diagnosed with Meniere's, I had a lot of questions but was given no answers. My ENT specialist handed me a simple folded leaflet and gave me two pieces of advice: walk away from stress and avoid salt. I asked him if there was a cure? 'No,' he said.

My recovery began with a decision: to do everything I could to *Get Better*. Once I made that decision, I focused on ways to beat Meniere's disease. I looked at all my Meniere symptoms and how they affected my physical, emotional, and mental wellbeing. I became mindful of my life with Meniere's. This mindful approach to Meniere's gave me the tools to recover from the 'incurable' Meniere's disease. My journey began with questions, but no answers. Remarkably, the answers I found ended in a full recovery. I also found quiet hope for others, suffering from Meniere's.

By living mindfully with Meniere's disease, I did more than one man fighting a disease, alone, was expected to do. I developed a Mindful Meniere Recovery Program, with real usable answers to questions about vertigo attacks, triggers, low salt diets, exercise programs, stress, anxiety, medication, vitamins, supplements, meditation, and alternative therapies such as acupuncture, and many more. I shunned options for surgical intervention and, contrary to prognosis, made a complete recovery.

Most people with Meniere's will have the same worries and questions as I had. But the main question everyone asks me, is how did Meniere Man get better? The answer to that critical question is always the same. Getting better starts with the belief that you can and will make a full recovery from Meniere's.

In the book of life, answers are not at the back end. Start now.

ANSWERS I WISH I WAS GIVEN WHEN DIAGNOSED

Question: *What Questions did you ask yourself?*

Answer: *How do I make a new life with the condition? Can I get better? Will I be able to function dynamically again? Will my relationships completely change now? Will we lose our financial position? How do we survive?*

Question: *If someone was recently diagnosed with Meniere's, what are five things you would tell them?*

Answer:
First: *accept the condition. It's not easy, but once you acknowledge the disease, you can begin to manage your health.*

Secondly: it is to have a belief in yourself that you can and will get better. Keep fanning a flame of hope in your mind.

Thirdly: because you are the one who needs to make a recovery, accept responsibility for getting better.

Fourthly: adopt a very positive attitude and keep as many aspects of your life positive.

Fifthly: gain information about Meniere's because knowledge is vital. You should spend as much time learning about Meniere's disease, as you spend worrying about it. There are now books, websites, Meniere support groups, and Meniere societies, as well as medical sites, and public libraries to help you learn more about Meniere's.

Question: Is every person's experience with Meniere's the same?

Answer: Meniere's disease affects people differently. Your experience may be different from my own. My experience was frequent acute (severe) rotational vertigo attacks, while other sufferers experienced less frequent acute vertigo attacks, others reported less severe attacks and were able to continue working.

Question: What are the symptoms of classic Meniere's disease?

Answer:
1: Episodic fluctuating rotational vertigo (spinning).

2: Episodic and fluctuating tinnitus (a sound heard when there is no sound).

3: *Episodic and fluctuating aural fullness (a sensation of pressure in the ear).*

4: *Episodic and fluctuating hearing loss.*

Question: *What is the Meniere's triad?*

Answer: *The clinical triad in Meniere's consists of three main symptoms: vertigo, tinnitus, and hearing loss.*

Question: *What are episodic Meniere's disease symptoms?*

Answer: *Episodic symptoms are aural fullness, tinnitus, and disabling rotational vertigo. As the word indicates, they can appear unprovoked at any time.*

Question: *What are fluctuating symptoms?*

Answer: *When symptoms fluctuate, they vary in intensity and duration. During an attack, hearing loss may fluctuate, vertigo severity may be more or less. After the attack, your hearing loss may be severe but returns to normal levels a few hours later. Tinnitus may be louder before, during, or after an attack. Most every episode is unpredictable, which makes no one attack the same. Symptoms can be more intense or less than the previous attack.*

Question: *Is there any known cure for Meniere's disease?*

Answer: *Unfortunately, there is no known cure for Meniere's disease. No one drug, and no one surgical procedure.*

Question: *Does no known cure mean you can never get better?*

Answer: *No cure means there are no medicines, drugs, or specific treatments to cure the condition, but that doesn't mean there isn't any way to get better. Using medication and a self-management program, I made a full recovery from Meniere's disease.*

Question: *Is Meniere's disease the same as Meniere's syndrome?*

Answer: *No. Meniere's disease has no known cause, whereas Meniere's syndrome (also known as endolymphatic hydrops) is caused by a specific condition. Meniere's syndrome: can occur due to various processes interfering with the normal production and absorption of endolymph, e.g. endocrine abnormalities, trauma, electrolyte imbalance, autoimmune diseases, lupus, rheumatoid arthritis (which may cause inflammatory responses within the inner ear), thyroid antibodies, infection, metabolic disturbances, hormonal imbalance, medications, parasitic infections, allergens, hyperlipidemia, and food allergies. If a cause is identified, then you have Meniere's syndrome, not Meniere's disease.*

Question: *How can you prevent Meniere's disease?*

Answer: *There is no known prevention for Meniere's disease. Meniere's symptoms develop without a known cause.*

Question: *What is the difference between dizziness and Meniere's disease?*

Answer: *Dizziness is a term used to describe feeling dizzy, faint, or lightheaded. This dizziness can cause you to be unsteady on your feet, stagger, or fall about, whereas the Meniere's disease experience is extreme rotational vertigo where one is unable to stand.*

Question: *What is the difference between general vertigo and Meniere's disease vertigo?*

Answer: *General vertigo is a sensation of an individual's surroundings moving. Meniere's vertigo is rotational spinning.*

Question: *Can you have Meniere's disease without vertigo?*

Answer: *No. To be diagnosed with Meniere's, one must experience uncontrolled episodic rotational vertigo, as one of the symptoms.*

Question: *Is labyrinthitis the same as Meniere disease?*

Answer: *No. Labyrinthitis symptoms can be similar to Meniere's, but they are two different conditions. Labyrinthitis is an inflammation of the inner ear that can cause episodes* of dizziness, associated nausea and vomiting, eye nystagmus, possible hearing loss, and ringing in the ears. It is also known as vestibular neuritis, caused by a virus, bacterial infection, stress, allergy, reaction to medication, or a head injury. Labyrinthitis can last for weeks, whereas Meniere's goes on for years.

Question: *What causes Meniere's disease?*

Answer: *There have been many theories but no known cause. Meniere's disease is constantly being re-evaluated.*

Question: *What part of the ear is affected by Meniere's Disease?*

Answer: *It affects the inner ear.*

Question: *What happens when the inner ear is affected by Meniere's?*

Answer: *When you have Meniere's, fluid builds up in the endolymphatic sac until the membrane that separates the chambers ruptures and floods the nerve of balance, creating a Meniere vertigo attack. Each time you have an attack, the small cilia in the inner ear are damaged, which results in a progressive hearing loss. Eventually, the affected ear is left with a degree of permanent hearing loss and tinnitus.*

Question: *What does fluid in the inner ear do?*

Answer: *Fluids plays an essential role in balance.*

Question: *What is a healthy inner ear?*

Answer: *The inner ear is a group of connected passages known as the labyrinth. The soft structure of the membrane is called the membranous labyrinth. The fluid contains a membranous structure called the endolymphatic sac. In a normal healthy ear, fluids in the endolymphatic sac are constantly being secreted and reabsorbed, maintaining a constant level of fluid.*

Question: *What is unilateral Meniere disease?*

Answer: *Unilateral is the term where Meniere's affects one ear. The majority of Meniere's patients are unilateral.*

Question: *Was your Meniere's unilateral?*

Answer: *Yes.*

Question: *Can you get Meniere's in the other ear?*

Answer: *Some sufferers are bilateral, (having Meniere's in both ears), or become bilateral at a later date.*

Question: *What are the chances of getting Meniere's in both ears?*

Answer: *The risk of developing the disease in the opposite ear is, unfortunately estimated to be as high as thirty percent.*

Question: *When is bilateral Meniere's disease likely to happen?*

Answer: *Most doctors believe that if you are going to suffer bilateral Meniere's, the symptoms will usually occur in the unaffected ear within two to five years from the onset of Meniere's in the first ear.*

Question: *Do the kidneys have a role to play in Meniere's?*

Answer: *The kidneys, and associated hormones produced by unhealthy kidney function, are thought to be involved in Meniere's onset. Drinking too much alcohol, overeating greasy sweet or spicy food, and too much processed food, all affect the kidneys adversely.*

Question: *What famous people today have Meniere's?*

Answer: *Famous people who have (or are thought to have) Meniere's are David Alstead - pianist, Steve Francis - professional basketball player - Dana Davis - author, Mike Reilly - American League, Ryan Adams, Katie Le Clerc - television and movie actor, Andrew Knight - editor, journalist and media baron, the late Les Paul - jazz guitarist, Jessica Williams - American pianist and composer, Kristen Chenoweth - American singer, musical theatre, film and television actress and author. Meniere's is not selective about who suffers it.*

Question: *What is the Tullio phenomenon in Meniere's disease?*

Answer: *Tullio phenomenon happens when a change in pressure sets off dizziness, nausea, and involuntary eye movement. Nose-blowing, swallowing, straining to lift heavy objects, loud music, or even the sound of your voice can set off vertigo, imbalance, and eye movement, hearing loss, and tinnitus. Meniere's syndrome is the most common cause of the Tullio phenomenon.*

Question: *Is Meniere's a debilitating disease?*

Answer: *Attacks of Meniere's are incredibly debilitating. At the time of rotational vertigo, you must lay down. The spinning sensation can be violent. Nausea, vomiting, sweating, and imbalance are all overwhelming and uncontrolled. So yes, the symptoms are debilitating.*

Question: *Is Meniere's a serious disease?*

Answer: *Meniere's disease is serious in its physical and mental effects, creating anxiety, depression, stress, tinnitus, and hearing loss. However, it is not a terminal disease.*

Question: *Is Meniere's a chronic condition?*

Answer: *Yes, it is, if the sufferer is experiencing unpredictable, and frequent attacks of vertigo, loss of balance, vomiting, dizziness, hearing loss, and severe tinnitus.*

Question: Is Meniere's disease fatal? Is Meniere's disease deadly? Is Meniere's terminal? Can you die from Meniere's?. Can Meniere's disease kill you?

Answer: These questions are the questions most asked. The answer to the big five is always the same. No, no, no, no, and no. Although during the darkest days of vertigo attacks when you might wish for a place in heaven, Meniere's is not terminal, and you won't die from it.

Question: Is Meniere's a progressive disease?

Answer: Meniere's is known to be a progressive disease with three stages.

Question: What is the classic first stage of Meniere's?

Answer: Stage one is the early onset of Meniere's disease, marked by unpredictable attacks of vertigo, fluctuating hearing loss, fullness feeling in the ear, and tinnitus.

Question: In stage one, what is the usual period between attacks?

Answer: In my case, the period between attacks could be hours, days or weeks. It varied. I couldn't see a pattern.

Question: What happened to your hearing?

Answer: I would have an increased feeling of fullness in

my ear, but after an attack, that all subsided, and the fullness disappeared.

Question: *What is stage two of Meniere's?*

Answer: *In stage two, vertigo attacks interrupt your life in unpredictable places and times. You experience increased tinnitus and a more profound progressive hearing loss.*

Question: *In stage two, did you have warnings of an attack?*

Answer: *After a few years, I recognized an increase in tinnitus, wooziness, and aural fullness. This pattern became well established and did precede an attack of vertigo.*

Question: *Was your Tinnitus worse during stage two?*

Answer: *Yes. Tinnitus became more intrusive and demanding.*

Question: *What is stage three of Meniere's?*

Answer: *Stage three is the late stage of Meniere's. Attacks of vertigo became less frequent and often less violent.*

Question: *What happened to your hearing in stage three?*

Answer: *Hearing loss became severe in the affected ear. Loud noises caused alarm. I soon experienced permanent hearing* *loss, and I found that initially rather depressing. Over the years, that devastating sense of loss became less.*

Question: *How long can Meniere's disease last?*

Answer: *Meniere's may persist for 30 years or more. Vertigo attacks can continue for decades.*

Question: *Can Meniere's go into remission?*

Answer: *Meniere's is an unpredictable illness. Meniere's disease is different for each person. You can experience temporary remissions, but the Meniere's will still be active.*

Question: *Can Meniere's burn out?*

Answer: *Yes, after several years, vertigo attacks may be less frequent and reduce in intensity. Hearing loss will stabilize at a moderate to severe level. Burn out often happens at the seven-year mark, but unfortunately, this is not the case for everyone.*

Question: *Does burning out mean Meniere's is cured?*

Answer: *Burning out doesn't mean Meniere's has gone or cured. It means hearing in the affected ear is permanently destroyed, and attacks have reduced in intensity, or have stopped altogether. I like to think for me, I will never suffer from Meniere's again, which, years later is thankfully true.*

Question: *When can I expect Meniere's disease to go away?*

Answer: *You will find no one can answer to timing. For me, Meniere attacks did go away after 4.5 years. I noted relief in intensity, and frequency of attacks in that time. However, my recovery was due to how I managed the condition by consistently applying, my mindful recovery strategies.*

Question: *Is Meniere's disease curable, or do you have Meniere's for life?*

Answer: *No, it's not curable. While there is no cure for Meniere's, you certainly can overcome Meniere's. I recovered fully by changing my lifestyle.*

Question: *Do you consider yourself lucky to have recovered from Meniere's?*

Answer: *I don't see the recovery I made as lucky. I worked out what might be exasperating the symptoms and the more I understood what was happening during attacks, the more I believed Meniere's could be managed effectively. For me, it was the determination to fully recover, that lead to my mindful recovery. I can't stress enough how much you can do to manage symptoms and recover your life. For me, this was the difference between suffering a long undetermined condition, or fully recovering into a healthy, empowered life.*

Question: *How bad can Meniere's disease get?*

Answer: *I had very bad days where I wouldn't have wished Meniere's on my worst enemy.*

Question: *What are the complications caused by Meniere's?*

Answer: *While Meniere's disease doesn't cause medical complications, it makes life distressing and challenging. Meniere's symptoms cause fear, lack of confidence, unreliability, and emotional stress. This can lead to anger, depression, and other psychological problems, which often need professional help.*

Question: *Why is smoking bad for Meniere's?*

Answer: *Smoking restricts blood vessels, which in turn affects the ability of blood to circulate efficiently in the inner ear. Limited blood flow restricts the amount of healing substances able to be delivered to your body, i.e., your ear. Your body is continually replacing itself on a cellular level, so ensure you have healthy blood.*

Question: *Is passive smoke bad for Meniere's?*

Answer: *Yes. Don't accept second-hand smoke. It's a health hazard that does you absolutely no good. Breathe in someone else's smoke, and you take into your body poisons and toxic chemicals.*

Question: *Does Meniere's disease cause fatigue?*

Answer: *Yes. Meniere damages the balance organ in the inner ear, which means the brain has to find ways to compensate for that loss of balance. The brain's compensation for balance is why you feel so tired. Also, physical, emotional, and mental fatigue are triggers for attacks, so fatigue is something you must manage.*

Question: *Did Meniere's make you tired?*

Answer: *Meniere's certainly made me dog-tired most of the time. I looked pale, drained of life, thoroughly washed out, and left without energy.*

Question: *What did you do when you felt tired?*

Answer: *I looked closely at myself, and when I felt tired, regardless of what I was doing, I stopped, and rested, or meditated. Relaxing sounds easy, but you have to take this very seriously.*

Question: *What things did you do to combat fatigue?*

Answer: *I stopped stacking one activity on top of the next. I learned that nothing was stamped urgent. I had to stop and spread the responsibilities. Once I did that, I noticed a significant reduction in attacks.*

Question: *Are headaches common with Meniere's disease?*

Answer: *Yes they are. If you are prone to headaches and migraines, you will experience an increase of Meniere symptoms.*

Question: *Did you get headaches with Meniere's?*

Answer: *Up to my diagnosis, I never rarely had headaches, but during the time of Meniere's, I went through headache medication like candy.*

Question: *What factors did you identify that triggered your Meniere's symptoms?*

Answer: *Stress, overwork fatigue, and salt.*

Question: *Did sinus or colds affect your Meniere's symptoms?*

Answer: *No. I didn't get sinus infections or suffer unduly with colds. I made an effort to avoid colds or flu by hand washing, avoiding contact with sick people, and taking a comprehensive regime of vitamins. I also took extra vitamins designed to increase health and resistance to colds at the change of seasons.*

Question: *Does barometric pressure and weather affect Meniere's symptoms?*

Answer: *Yes, it is well documented that Meniere's patients are sensitive to changes in weather. The fluid-filled inner ear is very sensitive to barometric pressure changes. For this reason, spring and fall are notably 'bad seasons' for sufferers. I only correlated barometric pressure with the onset of my attacks in the second stage of Meniere's.*

Question: *Did you ever feel lightheaded?*

Answer: *I call it woozy. Yes, most of the time.*

Question: *Does Meniere's cause memory loss?*

Answer: *Yes, Meniere's decreases memory retrieval.*

Question: *Is Meniere's disease brain fog real?*

Answer: *Brain fog is not a medical symptom used in diagnosing Meniere's disease. Brain fog is forgetting things, having trouble remembering, feeling disoriented, and confused. These symptoms are common when you suffer from a chronic medical condition. I experienced constant brain fog to different degrees in the early stages of Meniere's. But absolutely no brain fog since I recovered.*

Question: *Can Meniere's disease cause seizures?*

Answer: *While Meniere's disease doesn't cause seizures, it is a logical assumption that if you are prone to seizures, the effects of having Meniere's could exasperate seizure symptoms.*

Question: *What is your life expectancy if you have Meniere's disease?*

Answer: *Life expectancy is the same as if you didn't have Meniere's disease.*

Question: *What effect does Meniere disease have on the quality of life?*

Answer: *Research quantifies that people with Meniere's lose 43.9% from the optimum wellbeing position of normal people. In acute episodes, the wellbeing scale is recorded, as being at the same level found in patients facing terminal diseases, such as cancer.*

Question: *What is The Quality of Wellbeing Scale?*

Answer: *The Quality of Wellbeing Scale is a recognized scientific study applied to many aspects of human life. Meniere sufferers are the most severely impaired non-hospitalized patients studied. When Meniere's sufferers were not having acute attacks, Wellbeing was comparable to a very ill adult with a life-threatening illness. When a Meniere person was having acute attacks, the Wellbeing scale is closer to a person with Aids, or a Cancer patient...six days before death.*

Question: *What is the DHI?*

Answer: *The Jacobson's Dizziness Handicap Inventory (DHI) is a subjective test that helps a sufferer to explain the* impact vertigo is having on their life. It consists of twenty-five questions about vertigo, which measure the degree of physical, emotional, and functional disability.

Question: *What are the long-term effects of Meniere's?*

Answer: *After burnout, there will be moderate to severe hearing loss, chronic tinnitus, and ongoing balance issues.*

Question: *What are the long-term emotional effects?*

Answer: *I would say the trauma of having Meniere's affects your sense of wellbeing. One of the primary psychological effects is the loss of confidence in the present and the future.*

Question: *Does Meniere's disease make you stupid?*

Answer: *No, not that I have noticed, or that anyone has told me so far!*

Question: *Can Meniere's cause cognitive issues?*

Answer: *Yes. Cognitive issues persist while Meniere's is active. Meniere sufferers show a decreased ability to multitask, which shows as confusion, trouble keeping track of the relevant subject in a conversation, marked decrease in mental stamina, and memory recall. Meniere's also makes it difficult to grasp whole concepts. However, once the condition has decreased, cognitive issues don't continue. In fact after recovery you feel normal again with no lingering deficit.*

Question: *What makes Meniere's disease symptoms flare up and get worse?*

Answer: *No one knows for sure, but there are now numerous, well-documented known 'triggers' that can exasperate symptoms, like too much salt, stress, flickering lights, coffee, and chocolate. If you follow Meniere threads, you will find an extensive list of what sufferers feel trigger attacks. Keeping a personal diary of attacks and possible causes of the attack (triggers), helps clarify what aggravates your symptoms. The more aware you are of possible causes, the more you can avoid attacks.*

Question: *Can kidney function affect Meniere's symptoms?*

Answer: *According to traditional Oriental medicine, the kidneys influence the ears and hearing. If your kidneys are weak, then the normal functioning of your ears will be affected. The kidneys can only be nourished by the right nutrition. So you can stabilize the kidneys by eating well, giving you a robust kidney system. A strong, healthy system will help dizziness and tinnitus.*

Question: *Can Meniere's make you depressed?*

Answer: *Yes, it sure can. Changes in mood are common and for a good reason. Meniere's brings a lot of complications, discomfort, and loss of wellbeing. Some people find they need to take a course of prescribed antidepressants or anti-anxiety medication. Some seek counsel with a health professional.*

Question: *What did you do about depression?*

Answer: *On 'dark days', I talked to a professional about how Meniere's was adversely affecting my life.*

Question: *What other mood changes can happen?*

Answer: *Often, anger, irritability, fear, anxiety, impatience, and a lack of confidence come with Meniere's.*

Question: *What brought out your pessimistic side?*

Answer: *Not participating fully in social life, family, work, or sport. And an overwhelming fear of non-recovery.*

ANSWERS ON HOW TO MANAGE MENIERE'S

Question: *How did you manage Meniere's disease symptoms?*

Answer: *I took a self-help approach and looked at many factors, including prescription medicines, stress, diet, exercise, supplements, and mindful wellness. I then established my recovery program.*

Question: *What are triggers?*

Answer: *A trigger is something that causes certain symptoms to occur. I eliminated attacks of Meniere's disease, and I attribute this partly to recognizing and working with triggers. Firstly I worked on a list of possible things that might affect my symptoms. I then learned to recognize triggers that either induced attacks or made the attacks more intense. When I identified a trigger, I could avoid the trigger, and over time, this* helped to reduce the number of attacks. The attacks themselves became less intense and didn't last as long. Then I became attack free.

Question: *Explain why you kept a Meniere's disease diary?*

Answer: *Pen and paper are mighty tools for recovery. In the early days of Meniere's, I went out and bought a diary, tan leather. Just the simple act of journaling and writing daily (without missing a day), gave me a great sense of being in control. Keeping a journal was the beginning of the self-monitoring, and self-management needed to overcome Meniere's and get better.*

Question: *What did you write in your diary?*

Answer: *I wrote down what I did every day; this allowed me to go back after an attack and look at what I had done over the previous days. What had I been doing? What did I eat? What gave me stress? Did I drink alcohol? Argue? Have a late-night? I wrote down everything. I figured out what might be causing the attacks. My list of possible triggers was long. I wrote down the length of the attack, and the time frames between attacks.*

Question: *Were your diaries useful in your recovery?*

Answer: *Certainly. These diaries helped in my recovery, I am sure. Even the simple act of self-reflection, self-observation,* and recalling what you do, helped me become more mindful. By recording what was happening, I was able to see a clear past history of events and symptoms. This helped me accurately focus on past events and make adjustments to my diet, fitness, and stress management. Keeping a diary of Meniere's puts you in control of you life, so Meniere's is not controlling you.

Question: *What happened to your diaries?*

Answer: *The material was extremely useful. It was a record of my life with Meniere's and proved to be useful in writing books on Meniere's. I could see what I did to get better without surgery or invasive procedures. It was fundamentally apparent: there is a lot you can do to help yourself get better. I am a great believer that you can achieve anything you set your mind and heart on. My specialist encouraged me to write a book about self-management from a sufferers' point of view. Eventually, I took the manuscript into his office, and he endorsed my first book. I am grateful to him because he was upfront, honest and never pushed surgery as the option. Now the notes have been replaced by a series of books.*

ANSWERS TO VERTIGO MANAGEMENT

Question: *What gives us our sense of balance?*

Answer: *The balance system is made up of three senses that feed information to the brain: eyes, muscles, joints, feet, plus the vestibular organ.*

Question: *Why does Meniere's disease affect balance?*

Answer: *Meniere's adversely affects the vestibular system, which is one of our main balance mechanisms.*

Question: *What happens to your balance system?*

Answer: *The vestibular system receives sensory information, such as motion, equilibrium, and spatial orientation. The vestibular system is also responsible for transmitting this co-ordinated information to the brain. Active*

Meniere's damages the vestibular system, which inhibits balance information being sent to the brain. That is why you end up with balance problems.

Question: When Meniere spinning symptoms occur, what is it called?

Answer: It is called an 'attack'.

Question: Do you get warnings of a vertigo attack?

Answer: Yes. Any of the following symptoms indicate the beginning stage of a vertigo attack: Increased tinnitus/loud roaring, aural fullness, increased tiredness/yawning for no apparent reason, feeling off-balance, and decreased hearing. These symptoms mean the Reissner membrane is already being stretched by fluid build up in one of the endolymphatic sacs. These symptoms can build up over a day or two, or happen suddenly within half an hour.

Question: Did symptoms always warn you of an impending vertigo attack?

Answer: Yes. Symptoms became my essential tools for managing my attacks.

Question: Can you describe a typical warning of an attack?

Answer: *There was often an aura where some (or all) of the following specific symptoms warned me of an oncoming vertigo attack. Before an attack, I would feel less stable, experiencing a slight loss of balance, along with a woozy feeling or lightheaded. Sometimes I would get a crashing headache. I always noticed a sensation of increased pressure in the ear, as if my ear was stuffed with cotton wool. External sounds became more muffled. As tinnitus increased, hearing decreased.*

Question: *Why is it important to recognize the symptoms of a vertigo attack?*

Answer: *The sooner you recognize this beginning stage, the better. If you take action, you can avoid the attack or lessen the intensity. Whatever you do, consider this beginning stage seriously. If you are experiencing the beginning symptoms of a Meniere's vertigo attack, you need to put measures in place immediately, like resting mentally and physically for a day or two.*

Question: *Are nausea and vomiting symptoms of Meniere's disease?*

Answer: *No, nausea and vomiting are symptoms of many diseases, but not actual symptoms of Meniere's disease; rather, they are caused by rotational vertigo, which is a Meniere symptom. Feeling nauseous and vomiting are symptoms of a vertigo attack.*

Question: *What happens during a vertigo attack?*

Answer: *In the beginning, you experience severe dizziness, which quickly develops into nystagmus, where your eyes feel like they're following the room moving around you, but you are still mobile enough to find a place to lie down. After that, you are into an acute rotational spinning vertigo attack where you cannot move. Vertigo will last for at least thirty minutes to an hour.*

Question: *How did you cope with Meniere's attacks?*

Answer: *Once I understood what was happening during the attacks, I was able to reduce my stress. This knowledge gave me a sense of control. I recognized the beginning, middle, and end of each attack. Then I figured out what I could do at every stage to help myself manage the effects of the Meniere attack. The knowledge and management resulted in the attacks becoming less violent and less frequent, until I no longer had attacks at all.*

Question: *How does the Meniere attack finish?*

Answer: *Towards the end of the attack, you will notice the spinning is a little less severe. As the spinning slows down, you are managing to see something specific in the room, before it spins away. Slowly you can focus on a spot or a picture. Once you can focus on an object, the end of the episode is only a matter of time. Finally, there is no more spinning, and you can sleep.*

Question: *Are the intensity of attacks all the same?*

Answer: *No. The intensity at one end can be mild: feeling woozy, lightheaded, and a little unstable. At the other end of the scale, it's a spinning nightmare.*

Question: *How often do attacks happen?*

Answer: *Attacks vary in frequency. They can often happen as much as one every three days. I've had what I describe as cluster attacks. These happen every few days and go on like this for two or three weeks.*

Question: *How long does an attack last?*

Answer: *Meniere's disease symptoms come on as episodes or attacks. Symptoms vary in frequency and intensity, and can last from twenty minutes to one hour.*

Question: *Can one attack be followed by another?*

Answer: *Unfortunately, yes. You can have weeks where one attack is followed by another, with in the next day or two.*

Question: *Did you have days when you felt your Meniere's was getting worse?*

Answer: *Yes. Before I put my mindful recovery strategy in place, I was in the grips of uncontrolled, unpredictable vertigo attacks. Meniere's took over my life.*

Question: *What do you mean by 'wooziness'?*

Answer: *'Wooziness' describes a sense of imbalance.*

Question: *What is a drop attack? Did you experience this?*

Answer: *I never had a drop attack. I understand it feels like being suddenly pushed to the floor from behind.*

Question: *Did you ever have a Meniere attack while sleeping?*

Answer: *Yes. I experienced several vertigo attacks that woke me up from sleep.*

Question: *When is Meniere's disease the worst?*

Answer: *For me, it was often worse in the late afternoon.*

Question: *What is Meniere's 'window of opportunity'?*

Answer: *The time between episodes where symptoms are manageable. This period is what I call the 'window' of opportunity. A chance to do as much as you can towards your recovery. The time to do positive things for health: paying attention to diet, exercise, and reducing stress. One may not feel fantastic, but if you are careful, you can be productive and do normal day-to-day activities. The key is to maximize every opportunity to improve health.*

ANSWERS TO MEDICAL MANAGEMENT

Question: Is Meniere's disease considered to be a neurological problem?

Answer: No, it's not a neurological problem. Meniere's disease affects the inner ear and balance system. Therefore, it's considered to be a problem of the ear, treated by an Ear, Nose and Throat specialist.

Question: Who is the best doctor for Meniere's disease?

Answer: In my case, my general practitioner referred me to an Ear Nose and Throat (ENT) specialist who knew about Meniere's disease. The ENT specialist turned out to be the best person for me.

Question: What was the most significant thing your specialist told you?

Answer: *As far as management of Meniere's disease from a patient perspective, there wasn't a lot to tell me at the time, except he did say to give up salt and walk away from stress. What he said made me wonder what other things I should walk away from and give up.*

Question: *How is Meniere's disease treated medically?*

Answer: *There are many possible treatments for the symptoms of Meniere's, from out-patient procedures, vestibular balance training and/or surgery, plus of course, medications.*

Question: *What is gentamicin treatment?*

Answer: *It's an out-patient procedure where gentamicin is injected into the eardrum. The objective of the treatment is to destroy the endolymph. The endolymphatic sac is the immune organ of the inner ear. The theory of immune involvement in Meniere's disease has created a trend towards procedures aimed at destroying the endolymphatic sac. I understand you can expect four of these injections administered over a month, and this will stop vertigo for about a year. If the dizziness returns, expect another series of gentamicin injections.*

Question: *Did you consider gentamicin injections?*

Answer: *No. I understood it destroyed the ear. However, the use of intratympanic steroid injections has gained popularity over gentamicin, for treating Meniere's disease. Not all surgeons recommend it, as it is still a relatively new procedure, and the* *long-term effectiveness and side effects are not well documented.*

Question: *What is shunt surgery for Meniere's disease?*

Answer: *Lymphatic Sac Shunt is an out-patient procedure thought to preserve hearing and relieves vertigo. The probability of needing to repeat the operation is high because the shunt has a tendency to become blocked and needs replacing. The shunt is a procedure rated by some as having no more benefit than doing nothing at all.*

Question: *Was shunt surgery a procedure you considered?*

Answer: *My ENT surgeon did explain the operation to me, but I didn't consider having surgery as part of my mindful recovery strategy. So much is unknown about the condition, so treatments vary depending on the surgeon, or specialist, each having a preferred method for treating Meniere's. Surgeons are constantly changing views on surgical procedures for Meniere's. At this time, there appears to be no ultimate surgical answer.*

Question: *What is vestibular neurectomy?*

Answer: *Vestibular Neurectomy is the surgical cutting of the vestibular nerve (nerve of balance). Severing the nerve of balance, stops the balance information, from being transmitted to the brain.*

Question: *Did you consider vestibular neurectomy?*

Answer: *Never. Vestibular neurectomy is invasive radical surgery, and I was not into that idea at all. I found the idea of invasive surgery frightening. I prefer to take matters into my own hands, to retain control over outcomes. My friend went through this surgery. The procedure resulted in serious problems for him. He still had Meniere's, which went bilateral a year after the surgery.*

Question: *Did you have any surgery or medical procedures?*

Answer: *I chose to avoid all surgery and invasive procedures. I decided to self-manage the condition instead. For me, this proved to be the right thing to do. But in the end, it's a personal choice.*

Question: *What would you say to someone planning or contemplating surgery?*

Answer: *Regardless of acute symptoms, I'd say, don't rush into what may seem to be an easy or quick solution. If you're considering surgery, ask questions about the associated risk, prognosis, and success rate of the specific surgery.*

Question: *Should you get a second opinion?*

Answer: *Yes, for sure. Get a second and third medical opinion for treatment. I am adamant about this. It is a serious decision for you to consider.*

Question: *Did you ever think of surgery or procedures as a quick cure?*

Answer: *No. Not for me. It comes down to a personal choice. But I have met several people who had surgery hoping for a quick 'cure,' only to see them years later battling Meniere symptoms again. Most of these people were understandably embittered. However, they were still seeking and needing an end to Meniere's.*

Question: *If you didn't opt for surgery, what did you do?*

Answer: *I took two prescribed medications, and embarked on a holistic approach to getting well, which included lifestyle changes, low-salt diet, increased exercise, stress management, natural remedies, and meditation. The holistic management of Meniere's worked well for me. It was not a quick fix, and it didn't happen overnight. But it did work, and now I no longer have Meniere's disease.*

Question: *What are the new treatments for Meniere's?*

Answer: *The medical profession is continually trying new procedures in its effort to find treatments. Will the medical profession in the future agree one surgical or medical procedure? That is still the big question. Everyone involved in Meniere's is waiting to see.*

Question: *Can Meniere's disease be treated naturally?*

Answer: *There is no proven cure for Meniere's. However, Meniere's disease symptoms can be managed by using medication, vitamins, supplements, meditation, acupuncture, breathing techniques, exercise, and stress management.*

ANSWERS TO MEDICATION MANAGEMENT

Question: *What medications did you take for Meniere?*

Answer: *I took two drugs on a daily basis: a fluid pressure suppressant (diuretic) and an anti-nausea drug.*

Question: *Which diuretic did you take?*

Answer: *My Specialist prescribed Serc (Betahistine dihydrochloride).*

Question: *How does Serc help Meniere's?*

Answer: *It's thought to reduce the pressure in the inner ear, reducing the episodes of Meniere attacks.*

Question: *Was Betahistine useful for you?*

Answer: *Some people question its effectiveness. However, I found that if I missed a dose, I'd experience increased tinnitus, and feel woozy. And that often ended in an attack. Those symptoms were enough to make me stay on this medication until I was better.*

Question: *What diuretic did you take?*

Answer: *I took Kaluri, the brand name for the chemical Amiloride. It increases urinary output, which in turn flushes out sodium (salt). Amiloride is prescribed as a preferred diuretic because it retains potassium in the body.*

Question: *What are the side effects of a non-potassium sparing diuretic?*

Answer: *Diuretics can cause a loss of potassium, so it is essential to take a potassium supplement. Potassium assists the proper functioning of the kidneys, heart, nerves, and digestive system. Diuretics taken longer than six months can dramatically reduce levels of folic acid in the body. Lack of folic acid creates a toxic amino acid associated with the hardening of arteries. If you suffer from high cholesterol, take a folic acid supplement.*

Question: *What medications did you take for an acute vertigo attack?*

Answer: *For nausea and vomiting, I would take Stemitol, an anti-nausea drug used in the treatment of acute Meniere attacks. I took a tablet as soon as an attack started in an attempt to minimize the spinning sensation and nausea.*

Question: *Did you ever need a shot of Stemitol?*

Answer: *Only once, I was given a shot of Stemitol during a severe Meniere attack, which gave me huge relief.*

Question: *Did you ever go to the emergency department during an acute vertigo attack?*

Answer: *One night, before I was diagnosed with Meniere's, my partner rang the A&E department and reported my symptoms of severe dizziness. The A&E advised she bring me down, but I was too ill to go anywhere. So she rang the ambulance, and a paramedic team turned up. After examining me, they concluded it was a middle ear problem. Following that vertigo attack, I went to a specialist who diagnosed me as having Meniere's.*

Question: *Did you take painkillers?*

Answer: *I didn't need to take regular painkillers for Meniere's disease symptoms.*

Question: *Did you take over the counter medicine for Meniere's disease?*

Answer: No.

Question: Did you try any antiviral medications such as Zofran, Zoloft, Xanax, or Zyrtec for Meniere's disease?

Answer: No, I didn't take any antiviral medication.

Question: Any other medications such as Meclizine, Orthokine, or Klonopin?

Answer: No, just the ones I outlined previously. Drugs mask the problem and, in no way, solve it. Meclizine is often prescribed, but this medication only inhibits the central nervous system and inhibits neural transmission to the vestibular system, which could make balance worse.

Question: What is oto-104 for Meniere's disease?

Answer: Increasing evidence implicating autoimmunity in Meniere's disease, has seen the steroid oto-104 gain in popularity, over gentamycin.

Question: Did you take steroids to help treat Meniere's?

Answer: Personally speaking, I didn't want steroids as part of my management system. However, corticosteroids, by their anti-inflammatory and immunosuppressive action, are becoming popular as a method for controlling vertigo.

Question: Do you take medication now you are well?

Answer: *I don't take any medications now. When I was symptom-free, my specialist told me I would need to take Serc for the rest of my life. I wasn't happy about that. So once I felt better, after a great deal of thought, I cautiously reduced the Serc dosage down, cutting the tablets into tiny quarters until I was off the drug altogether. Mind you, I don't advocate going against doctor's orders; it was a personal choice I made, to be off all medications.*

ANSWERS TO MENIERE'S DIET

Question: What food allergies did you have?

Answer: I have never suffered from any food allergies.

Question: What diet do you recommend for Meniere's?

Answer: I did follow the principles of the Zone Diet. I ate six small meals a day to keep blood sugar levels up, I increased servings of vegetables, both raw, and cooked and added flaxseed oil to my diet. I added more fresh fruit than The Zone Diet allowed. I used The Zone Diet as a template for healthy eating; more fiber, less processed food, avoided empty carbohydrates, ate lean meats, had less sugar and ate an abundance of fresh vegetables. It's healthy eating, without salt.

Question: *Did you follow The Paleo Diet?*

Answer: *I inadvertently followed their recommendations for grains, low sugar, low salt, less processed foods.*

Question: *What are the general rules for food?*

Answer: *Eat well-balanced meals. Don't skip meals. Eat low fat, low sugar, low salt snacks. Severely limit salt, alcohol, and caffeine. Eat fresh fruit and vegetable and less processed foods.*

Question: *Why is a low salt diet recommended for Meniere's disease?*

Answer: *Excess sodium creates fluid retention, which creates an imbalance in the body's fluids, especially in the inner ear. Fluid volume can trigger vertigo. So one goal for managing Meniere's vertigo is to reduce the total body fluid volume by avoiding substances that may trigger or exacerbate fluid pressure build up in the inner.*

Question: *What is a low sodium diet for Meniere disease?*

Answer: *According to the University of Maryland Medical Centre, maintaining a low salt diet involves restricting sodium intake to between 1,500 to 2,000 milligrams per day. I would aim for between 500 to 1000 mg per day.*

Question: *What low salt measures did you take?*

Answer: *Adding salt must be the first habit you give up. Avoid adding salt to food while cooking. Don't add salt to meals at the table. Throw away sauces in bottles; they are all very high in salt and sugar. No preserved meat products. One sausage maybe your entire salt intake for the day. Even bread has high salt content. One of the best ways to change an eating habit is not to have high salt items in the house. When eating out, I asked for no salt and avoided meals with sauces. Initially, I kept a tally of my salt intake every day, until I educated myself on their salt content. I still read salt content of products before I buy.*

Question: *Can you cut out all salt?*

Answer: *No salt is not necessary or advisable. Don't try to eliminate salt, your muscles and nerves need it to function. For more information, talk to a dietitian or nutritionist.*

Question: *Where are hidden salts found in foods?*

Answer: *A general low salt rule, avoid or limit processed foods that are high in sodium; canned vegetables, soups, spaghetti sauce, most sauces in a can or bottle, ketchup, vegetable juices, and ready to eat cereals. Avoid canned ravioli, salted nuts, potato crisps, broth, bouillon cubes, and gravies. The list goes on. You will be surprised when you run a salt count over your food intake for the day.*

Question: *How can I shop low salt?*

Answer: *Many choices of low salt foods are available in supermarkets, food stores, and markets. It's easy to replace high salt foods with low salt foods. Here's an example. Instead of crackers with high salt content, choose a brand with low salt content. You can still eat foods you love; you just have to put low salt products into your shopping trolley.*

Question: *Can you still eat out and do take-outs?*

Answer: *Yes you can, but you need to ask for no salt or MSG when you order and avoid dishes with sauces, like black bean sauce, soy sauce, and chili sauce in Asian restaurants. Don't reach for the sauces on the table.*

Question: *What is the difference between sodium and salt?*

Answer: *Sodium is the chemical name for salt. Food producers use the name Sodium on their product labels.*

Question: *How much salt in a low salt diet?*

Answer: *You know you need to eat healthily on a low salt diet, but how do you do it? Well, the first thing is to know how much daily sodium (salt) intake there is on a low salt diet. A low salt diet is 400 -1000 mg of salt a day. A normal salt diet is 1100 – 3300 mg a day. A high salt diet is 4000 - 6000 mg a day. Maintaining a sodium intake below 2000 mg a day takes effort.*

Initially, you can try to reduce salt levels to 1000 - 2000 mg a day, and see if there is any improvement. You may be fine at that level, or you can cut it to 500 -1100 mg a day. There is no need to be afraid of salt; you just need to control the intake. To maintain a low salt diet, you need to read the Nutritional Information printed by law, on the side of cans and packets of food.

Question: *What advice would you give to anyone starting on a low salt diet?*

Answer: *A low salt diet is key to reducing symptoms. Throw away the saltshaker! Don't add salt to cooking, And be vigilant at counting salt/sodium content on packaging. Write down your salt intake per day.*

Question: *Did you juice for Meniere's disease?*

Answer: *Yes. I ate or squeezed lemons, oranges, and limes for my vitamin C. I juiced beetroot, celery, apples, and carrots to create delicious vitamin-rich drinks.*

Question: *What about sugar and Meniere's?*

Answer: *Simple sugars are 'bad' sugars. Because almost as soon as you eat them, they cause a sugar high, followed by a sudden drop in blood sugar levels. This sudden spike and drop can trigger a Meniere's vertigo attack. Lowering the level of blood sugar in your body, is essential. Cut out simple carbohydrates and simple sugars from your diet. Instead, go for complex carbohydrates, like beans, wholemeal bread, brown rice,* vegetables, and high fiber foods, which are known to stabilize the body's blood sugar levels.

Question: *What sugar foods should you avoid with Meniere's disease?*

Answer: *The following foods should be reduced or eliminated from your diet; concentrated fruit juice, candy, cookies, biscuits, cakes, muffins, donuts, sweets, pasta and bread made with white flour, sugary cereals, white sugar, ice cream, milk chocolate. No jams, no soda drinks, or sauces in bottles or tins. Exclude preserved foods, such as olives, tinned fish, most cheeses, sausages and deli products. The food industry products are high in salt and sugar.*

Question: *What foods should you eat with Meniere's?*

Answer: *Basically, whole primary foods. Whole grain bread, brown rice, legumes like dried beans, pulses and lentils, vegetables, barley, wild rice, soybeans, fruits, nuts, and seeds, fish and meat. All of these complex carbohydrates have multiple benefits, and give you more energy. Not only do they taste great, but they are a perfect way to get the minerals and vitamins your body needs to heal.*

Question: *What was your favorite low salt meal?*

Answer: *Thin Italian spaghetti with a simmered sauce of Roma tomatoes, olive oil, garlic, and topped with ground black pepper, shredded fresh basil picked straight from the herb garden.*

Question: *What oils did you use?*

Answer: *I cooked with virgin coconut oil and olive oil. I used cold-pressed extra virgin olive oil and flaxseed oil in dressings. I also ate oily fish, giving me a high intake of Omega-3.*

Question: *Did you enjoy cooking for Meniere's?*

Answer: *Yes. I love good food. I cooked a lot of low salt Italian, Indian, and traditional European foods.*

Question: *Did Meniere's affect your weight?*

Answer: *No, not at all. I maintained a healthy weight through exercise and eating whole foods.*

Question: *Are bananas good for Meniere's disease?*

Answer: *Bananas are one of the richest sources of potassium and a convenient food source. Potassium-rich foods help the body control salt levels.*

Question: *How does potassium help Meniere's disease?*

Answer: *Potassium helps relieve blood pressure, anxiety, stress, and the nervous system. Many people take diuretics, and unless the medication is specifically potassium sparing, taking diuretics daily can cause potassium depletion in the body. Adding bananas to your diet can help with replacing lost potassium.*

Question: *What about plant sterols?*

Answer: *Eating well to get well involves using anti-inflammatory foods in your diet. Young green shoots of alfalfa, mung beans, and cress are all rich in plant sterols. These anti-inflammatory foods improve circulation to the inner ear.*

Question: *Is ginger good for Meniere's disease?*

Answer: *Ginger boosts the immune system. I found ginger tea made with grated ginger root, and boiling water helped to control the woozy feeling. Adding ginger to your diet stimulates circulation. Ginger also acts as an antiemetic to help with nausea. If you are taking blood thinner medication, check with your doctor to see if taking ginger is advisable.*

Question: *Are there natural diuretics for Meniere's disease?*

Answer: *Many foods that have a diuretic effect, such as apple cider vinegar, artichoke, asparagus, beets, Brussels sprouts, cabbage, carrots, cranberry juice, cucumber, green tea, fennel, lettuce, oats, and watermelon.*

Question: *Can green tea help with Meniere's disease?*

Answer: *Green tea is a natural diuretic and contains powerful antioxidants and bioflavonoids which are valuable to the Meniere's diet.*

Question: *What was your worst dining out experience?*

Answer: *Chinese chicken wonton soup. I asked for no salt with my order. The steaming noodle bowl arrived with wontons, but the broth tasted like oily bathwater. Without the usual MSG or salt, the dish tasted ghastly.*

ANSWERS TO FITNESS

Question: *Have you always been interested in sport?*

Answer: *Yes, I started playing football at seven years old and played sports all throughout my school years. I was a national competitive surfer; also I was involved in martial arts, scuba diving, windsurfing, and snowboarding.*

Question: *Did this stop with Meniere's?*

Answer: *I stopped martial art, and scuba diving, replacing it with Tai Chi.*

Question: *Does Meniere's limit physical activity?*

Answer: *Unless you're a circus performer, you can do most activities. Remember, the more you do, the more you can do.*

Question: *Does exercise help Meniere disease?*

Answer: *Yes. On so many levels, from increasing general fitness and balance to helping with recovery and maintaining a positive mental state.*

Question: *How soon after an attack would you do exercise?*

Answer: *As soon as I could, I walked, or practiced tai chi. Remember, exercise improves your balance and your attitude. Check with your doctor about how often and for how long you should exercise.*

Question: *Did you push your physical limits?*

Answer: *Always. You have to push forward. Every incremental step is an achievement, no matter how small. When you exercise more, you notice you can achieve more and balance better. That is how it goes.*

Question: *How frequently did you exercise?*

Answer: *If I wasn't having a vertigo attack, I walked and went to the gym five days a week. On the weekends I would do a sport like windsurfing, if I could.*

Question: *Did you exercise on bad days?*

Answer: *On bad days; I would take small steps, like walking around the garden or taking a stroll along the road. Exercise lifted my sense of ability, control, and recovery. Most days were bad days if I didn't exercise.*

Question: *Did exercise make you feel better?*

Answer: *Yes, by exercising, I could turn a bad day into a good day.*

Question: *Did you get relief from Meniere's symptoms?*

Answer: *I often had relief from symptoms; by the sea, in the countryside, exercising, meditating, or having an aromatherapy bath.*

Question: *Is boxing good for Meniere's?*

Answer: *Fitness boxing where you hit a punching bag, helps improve muscle strength, balance, stamina, and eye-hand coordination. Contact boxing is a bad idea. The last thing you need is a bang on the head.*

Question: *What is your pick of physical activities for Meniere's disease?*

Answer: *Walking and core training exercises. Both were essential to my recovery.*

Question: *Why is walking good?*

Answer: *Getting out of the house in the fresh air and walking is essential to living a healthy, independent life. Staying inside can lead to a downward spiral. After the vertigo attack is over, get up and go for a walk, even if it's just to the lamp-post. Regular walking exercise is key to maintaining and increasing circulation, strength, flexibility, and balance. Walking regularly maintains bone strength, and helps to improve balance.*

Question: *What was your best form of exercise?*

Answer: *Definitely walking. It was easy, simple, and didn't require anything much in the way of equipment, except good shoes. I used walking as a vital tool for my recovery. I measured distance and pace, increasing both whenever I was able.*

Question: *What was your least preferred form of exercise?*

Answer: *Tennis, because I'm no good at backhand anyway.*

Question: *Can you go running with Meniere's?*

Answer: *Keen runners often ask this question. If running is your sport, go for it, but if you feel unstable, you must walk or jog and run on the good days. Monitor your heartbeat.*

Question: *What are the two physical activities you had to give up with Meniere's?*

Answer: *Theme park rides and scuba diving.*

Question: *What sports can't you do with Meniere's?*

Answer: *Flying a plane, scuba diving and motor racing.*

Question: *Did you take up new physical activities?*

Answer: *Yes I did. Try was the word. I tried skiing, and took up snowboarding, tried wake-boarding, but spent more time windsurfing. I learned to use gym weights —the correct way.*

Question: *What was the most daring thing you did when you had Meniere's?*

Answer: *Scary rather than daring, I went up a ski gondola in high winds and snow-ploughed back down in a whiteout.*

Question: *What tested the limit of your sense of balance?*

Answer: *High places, escalators, balconies, glass lifts, and the edge of cliffs.*

Question: *You took up a lot of balance activities? Why?*

Answer: *I needed to develop my balance sensors, which proved to be right for me.*

Question: *Why are balance exercises so important?*

Answer: *Balancing activities help you regain equilibrium and confidence. You can learn balance exercises at home or in the gym. Practicing balance exercises regularly, encouraged me to learn snowboarding and windsurfing.*

Question: *Can balance exercises help Meniere's?*

Answer: *Most definitely. Tai chi, yoga, physical therapy, muscle strengthening, stretching, sport, all help balance. This, in turn, gives you confidence.*

Question: *Is core balance good for Meniere's?*

Answer: *The core muscles are in the hips, back, and abdomen. Strengthening these muscles helps with balance as they hold your body in an upright position and help with the coordination of the central nervous system.*

Question: *Are stretching exercises good for Meniere's disease?*

Answer: *Definitely. A stretching program for muscles of the calves, hamstrings, hip flexors, quadriceps, shoulders, and lower back helps to improve your range of motion and balance. When you have Meniere's, your body is in a constant state of* correcting balance, and this creates tension, especially in the neck and shoulders. I still do a stretching exercise program, three or four times a week.

Question: Are there vestibular balance exercises for Meniere's disease?

Answer: Vestibular rehabilitation (VR), or vestibular rehabilitation therapy (VRT) is an exercise program designed to help reduce vertigo and dizziness. It includes a series of specific exercises that train the brain to ignore the abnormal signals from the inner ear.

Question: Can you do yoga with Meniere's disease?

Answer: With any physical activity, you need to listen to your body and do what feels comfortable.

Question: Why is yoga good?

Answer: Yoga postures and breathing help reduce tension in the muscles and improve flexibility, essential for balance. It also promotes static balance without swaying.

Question: Why is tai chi good?

Answer: This ancient Eastern exercise improves balance, flexibility, and reduces anxiety.

Question: What was your favorite winter sports?

Answer: *Snowboarding.*

Question: *What were your favorite summer sports?*

Answer: *Windsurfing with my daughter, swimming in the ocean, and relaxing in a hammock.*

Question: *How was it possible to do balance sports?*

Answer: *I did comprehensive balance exercises and that gave me the confidence to learn more sports. If I felt even remotely dizzy, I wouldn't do them until I felt confident again.*

Question: *How did you utilize good days?*

Answer: *As soon as I had a good day, even for an hour or two, I would get up and get moving. If I began to feel unwell, I would stop the activity.*

Question: *Was doing balance activities a conscious decision?*

Answer: *I always liked balance activities. Even as a young boy, I loved balancing on a forty-four-gallon drum and making it roll around the garden. Without balance, life is physically crippling. Research has shown; that the more balance activities you do during the first six months of a diagnosis, the better the prognosis for balance recovery. However, there is no time like the present to begin, as there is no window of failure. Every day is a new day on the road to recovery.*

Question: *Did you take any physical risks with Meniere's?*

Answer: *Some activities were considered a little risky, such as windsurfing, surfing, and snowboarding. Most of the risk was thinking the activity was going to be too demanding. At one stage, I struggled to bend down and tie my shoelaces without feeling dizzy. It was hard to imagine doing demanding ones, but it was the will to get my life back from Meniere's that encouraged me to try.*

ANSWERS TO SUPPLEMENT MANAGEMENT

Question: *Why are nutritional supplements used for Meniere's disease?*

Answer: *Supplements balance your mineral and vitamin deficiencies. Tests revealed that people with Meniere's are usually low in iron, low in vitamin A, low in potassium, magnesium, and low in the Co-enzyme Q_{10}.*

Question: *What would you recommend as supplements?*

Answer: *My supplement regime was a quality multi-vitamin, vitamin C, B6 and B12, Coenzyme Q_{10}, magnesium, mainly to support immune functions and nerve recovery.*

Question: *Did you read up on vitamins and minerals?*

Answer: *Yes. As well as talking to nutritional therapists, I read books like Optimum Sports Nutrition, by Michael Colgan. The more you understand how essential, minerals and vitamins are for health, the sooner you'll achieve maximum health.*

Question: *Do you think vitamins and mineral supplements helped in your recovery?*

Answer: *I believe so. In the early stages of Meniere's, my body was deficient in vitamins, and my adrenals were down. I thought if I was going to step up my physical goals and improve my health, I needed to look at my vitamin and mineral intake.*

Question: *Is the quality of supplements important?*

Answer: *Certainly, It is important to read the small print to check the quantity of minerals and vitamins in each supplement.*

Question: *But vitamins and supplements can be expensive, how did you counter this?*

Answer: *I bought in bulk with good discounts from a reputable supplement importer, who delivered to my house. She was a nutrition expert who had recovered from a chronic condition using vitamins and supplements for healing, so she also shared a lot of useful information.*

Question: *What was your supplement regime?*

Answer: *With the help and guidance of nutritional professionals, and product information from health and wellness companies, I worked out the following personal vitamin and supplement regime. Note, this was my regime. Before taking on a vitamin regime, it is advisable to talk to your doctor. Many sufferers ask me for the Meniere Man supplement regime, so I have included it here for you.*

Vitamin C: *Vitamin C 2000 mg to 4000 mg spread throughout the day, and at least one hour before or after food. Vitamin C increases blood vessel permeability and allows red cells to mobilize. Vitamin C supports the kidneys, liver, and immune system.*

Vitamin E: *Increases blood vessel health and permeability, promotes healing, and is an antioxidant. 400 mg of vitamin E, twice a day, at mealtimes.*

EFA's: *Essential fatty acids are important for reducing inflammation and assisting in nerve transmission. Take a 300 mg salmon oil capsule, three times a day. Or flaxseed oil one teaspoon three times a day.*

Complex Vitamin B: *Complex B's assist in nerve regeneration. A Complex B tablet contains B6, B2, B5, B12, which are all clinically proven to assist the nervous system, reducing stress, depression, tension, and generally picking up your energy levels. B's also keep your immune system supported.*

Multi-vitamins: *When you take a multi-vitamin, you need to read the levels of vitamins in it and take that into account when you add the supplements you are taking. Choose a scientifically formulated multi-vitamin of high-quality, like Twin Labs, Swisse Men, Swisse Women. When you take a quality supplement, you can feel the difference.*

Potassium Sulfate: *85 mg once a day, replenishes potassium depletion in the body. It maintains and restores membrane potential and assists metabolic processes.*

Calcium supplement: *The supplement is for bone support, and it must contain Pantothenate 75 mg and Calcium Citrate 200 mg. Calcium also assists with sleep.*

Magnesium Citrate: *50 mg supports the nervous system.*

Question: *Why did you create a supplement booster regime?*

Answer: *Illness, medication, stress, and anxiety, all increase your body's need for essential minerals and vitamins. This means you need to, from time to time, give your system a boost with additional supplements for three-month periods throughout the year. I also took other vitamins that provided extra support for my adrenal glands and immune system all year round.*

Question: *What was your three-month booster regime?*

Answer: *In the early stages of Meniere's, in addition to* the daily vitamin regime, I would use the following supplements daily for three months.

Zinc: Strengthens the immune system, and improves cognitive function. Zinc also increases energy.

Oil of Primrose: EFA (essential fatty acid) Boosts your immune system and supports your nervous system.

Selenium: Keeps blood vessels healthy, reduces anxiety, depression, and improves the immune system.

Carnitine: A natural antioxidant; helps mood, memory, and cognitive ability; helps control blood sugar levels.

Chromium: 30 mg helps control cholesterol.

Co-enzyme: Q10: 50 mg, three times a day for 90 days. Q10 helps to improve vertigo symptoms, improves energy, assists memory, mood and builds resistance to stress, infection, and disease.

Silica: Encourages self-repair and healing to the immune and nervous systems. Facilitates the electrical balance of the cells; helps regenerate the liver and repair the body. Take liquid silica three times a day for three months.

Question: Now you no longer have Meniere's, do you take daily vitamins and mineral supplements?

Answer: I now just concentrate on eating a healthy diet with plenty of essential oils. But if my body is under stress, I take my booster regime.

Question: *Did you try ginkgo biloba?*

Answer: *Ginkgo is known to have a beneficial action on circulation, especially to the arterial circulation of the head. Ginkgo supplement is said to decrease tinnitus and dizziness by increasing blood flow to the head and therefore increasing circulation of the middle ear. I tried two capsules three times a day for two months to see if it helped my symptoms. I didn't recognize any change. If you take ginkgo, do not take with aspirin, also don't forget to check with your doctor before taking supplements.*

Question: *Is medical cannabis used to treat Meniere's disease symptoms?*

Answer: *I understand that medical cannabis can help well over 100 illnesses and diseases. However, my ENT specialist told me early on in my diagnosis, never to be involved in anything that affects your balance, and so I haven't. I avoided (and still do) substances that affect stability or balance, raise blood pressure, or may contain contaminants or unknown additives.*

Question: *Do you think vitamin D helps?*

Answer: *Vitamin D is essential for health. The best source of vitamin D is a 15-minute dose of sunshine. Sunlight in the morning is the best when it is called blue light. When you go for a walk, sunlight is absorbed through your eyes and becomes*

Vitamin D in your body, so it's important not to wear sunglasses or sunblock for fifteen minutes in the morning.

Question: *What supplements, if any, help with tinnitus?*

Answer: *Magnesium supplements help relieve tinnitus associated with Meniere's disease. Vitamin B12 supplements help sufferers who are deficient in this essential vitamin.*

ANSWERS TO WORK AND FINANCES

Question: *Should I let people know I have Meniere's?*

Answer: *Knowing what you are going through helps them to be more caring and to make allowances. You can be clear about what you can and can't do. As the disease develops, so your colleagues need to be updated about changes you need to make to your working day. If you explain that you have Meniere's and how it affects you, your employers and/or colleagues will hopefully show their supportive side. I didn't do this, and I think it created confusion. In retrospect, I would tell them.*

Question: *Can you work with Meniere's disease?*

Answer: *Being able to be employed with Meniere's and still perform at the level you used to, can be a problem. The fact is, you simply won't be able to take the stress or workload at the same level. You may have to negotiate your way to a lesser position with fewer demands. Hopefully, you can come to arrangements, as being socially included and financially independent in a time of Meniere's is essential.*

Question: *How does Meniere's affect working life?*

Answer: *Meniere's brings a new set of criteria for your health and your earning capacity. If you ignore the impact Meniere's is having on your life, your situation could escalate to the negative. From experience, the beginning stage is the time to make significant decisions to address changes Meniere's will bring, especially if you are the primary financial contributor to the family. Your health deficit may impact on your household, finances, and job. You must take all your living factors into account. If you do this with the help of family and professionals, your life won't fall into chaos because of Meniere's. The ideal position is to take your hands off the controls, but still be in control. You can solicit help from your partner, business colleagues, friends, and family.*

Question: *Could you multi-task?*

Answer: *I struggled to multi-task. It was a big issue for* me. I could only concentrate on one project at a time. And if the task was complicated, I struggled to come to grips with its dynamics.

Question: *Did you work with Meniere's disease?*

Answer: *At first, I tried to work, but I had such a high power job, I quickly fell behind. As an owner of a business, I would sit through meetings with clients plus meet production deadlines and then socialize with clients in the evenings. I couldn't keep the pace up. I suffered so many debilitating Meniere's attacks, and I soon ran out of excuses for my absences.*

Question: *Were you able to continue to work due to Meniere's disease?*

Answer: *I wasn't able to perform at the level expected of me, so I took a leave of absence from my business. I was never well enough to go back to work.*

Question: *Did you tell your colleagues you had Meniere's?*

Answer: *No. I kept it to myself, but when I sold my position in the business, my partners were aware of why I had to resign.*

Question: *Why couldn't you tell your business partners?*

Answer: *I didn't want to be seen as a weak link or socially handicapped or incapable. My ego, I suppose.*

Question: *Should you let work colleagues know you have Meniere's disease?*

Answer: *I think it is a good idea to let employers and people you work with know how this condition is affecting you. Looking back, I certainly wish I had done that.*

Question: *When you're ill, can you make big decisions?*

Answer: *Not on your own. Find help from professionals and people you trust. Look at one issue at a time and take the decision-making process slowly. Trust that you will always come up with suitable solutions.*

Question: *What suggestions do you have on maintaining an income stream?*

Answer: *If you are self-employed, look at options, like cutting down hours even if it means taking less money and/or hire someone to help you. Face this issue head-on, define, and clarify your position. If you are employed, use the support of professional people to advise you of your legal situation and options within your employment. Cut back on extra expenses. Fewer outgoings can create a surprising financial buffer.*

Question: *Do think it's a good idea to figure out options on your own?*

Answer: *My suggestion is to look around and seek advice on what to do from a variety of professional sources, arbitrators, counselors, and medical specialists. Use more than one source. Then go and talk with your employer or partners and work out a solution to the situation.*

Question: *Is income protection insurance helpful?*

Answer: *Socrates, the ancient Greek philosopher, once said, 'Security is the absence of awareness of danger.' Paddle your own canoe, and don't rely on disability insurance if you can help it. Make adjustments and keep control of your finances. Make sure you legally protect your existing assets. The law of the social jungle can be very aggressive and will take advantage, if you are not aware and protected.*

Question: *What is your advice to minimize the financial impact of Meniere's?*

Answer: *If I had fully understood Meniere's in the beginning, I would have taken time off work to restructure things, without it impacting and draining financial resources. A little less money, more time, and careful planning will give you a chance to survive financially.*

Question: *What impact did Meniere's have on your career?*

Answer: *At the time, I was running a multi-million dollar company. Meniere's signaled the end. The symptoms were* *so severe. Had I not had Meniere's, I would still be working at an international level.*

Question: *How did Meniere's change your life path?*

Answer: *I lost a successful business career because of Meniere's. The disease had a massive impact on the subsequent direction of my life. I countered this change by appreciating what was most important to me, my health and family. This is not groundbreaking news, but it seems to be the truth.*

ANSWERS TO TINNITUS

Question: *What is tinnitus? What causes ringing in Meniere's disease?*

Answer: *Tinnitus is the sensation of sound, buzzing and ringing in your ear. I initially went looking for the origin of my sudden tinnitus sounds, only to find the noise was coming from inside my head. Later I found it was all due to Meniere damage.*

Question: *What causes tinnitus in Meniere's?*

Answer: *Meniere's tinnitus is due to damaged nerve hairs in the inner ear. These damaged hairs send incomplete signals to the brain along the auditory nerve. Meniere people hear rushing ringing sounds.*

Question: *Is an increase in tinnitus sound a warning of a pending vertigo attack?*

Answer: *For me, yes. An attack followed a noticeable*

increase in tinnitus. Tinnitus increased when I was under stress, eating the wrong foods, or doing too much. I still use tinnitus as an early warning sign that my body is under stress and immediately back off activities and reflect on what I had just eaten or drunk.

Question: *Is tinnitus worse during a vertigo attack?*

Answer: *For me, tinnitus increased before a vertigo attack. During an attack, vertigo dominated me. I had no memory of tinnitus. However, other people do say tinnitus is markedly worse during the attack.*

Question: *Does tinnitus vary in sound?*

Answer: *Yes. There is a cacophony of sounds: ringing, hissing, static, crickets, screeching, whooshing, roaring, pulsing, ocean waves, buzzing, dial tones, and even music. The sound of chirping crickets is one of mine, along with the 747 jet engine whine. At one time, the crickets seemed to pack themselves into the 747. One can have any of these sounds.*

Question: *Can tinnitus affect both ears?*

Answer: *Tinnitus is brain activity and not the ear itself, but yet, the constant ringing (or another sound) may seem like it is coming from one ear or both.*

Question: *Is tinnitus the same for everyone?*

Answer: *I experienced tinnitus 24/7, and it only fluctuated louder before an attack. Other sufferers I spoke with experienced episodic tinnitus that went from extremely loud to not loud enough to bother them.*

Question: *Do hearing aids help cure tinnitus?*

Answer: *No. Hearing aids help you to hear sounds, but they won't cure tinnitus. New technology hearing aids can include 'blue-tooth' programs to give specific relief from tinnitus, (such as a white noise sound), which helps to mask an element of tinnitus. There are also tinnitus specialists who offer help for tinnitus.*

Question: *How did you cope with tinnitus?*

Answer: *I used the sound of tinnitus to warn me of an impending attack. It was useful in that regard, and helped me feel positive towards the ringing and rushing of tinnitus.*

Question: *Did you try alternative treatments for tinnitus?*

Answer: *I tried white noise, and acupuncture, none of which helped. I found meditation or music, helped me forget the tinnitus. Even a half-hour break from the noise was a relief.*

Question: *What seems to make tinnitus worse?*

Answer: *Salt, caffeine, alcohol, spicy foods, stress, and getting overtired. Even thinking about tinnitus made it worse.*

Question: *Can the Epley maneuver help with tinnitus?*

Answer: *No. The Epley maneuver can help ease positional vertigo, but won't do anything for tinnitus.*

Question: *What did you do that helped your tinnitus?*

Answer: *I accepted it for what it was. I stopped focusing on how bad it was. I realized the noise was not a threat or a danger to my physical person. The more I accepted tinnitus, the easier tinnitus was to live with.*

ANSWERS TO ALTERNATIVE THERAPIES

Question: *Which alternative medicine treatments did you try to help relieve symptoms of Meniere's disease?*

Answer: *I used a combination of natural therapies to help symptoms. Mind-body medicine such as breathing techniques, biofeedback, meditation, total body relaxation techniques, massage, acupressure, and acupuncture. Every alternative therapy comes down to a personal choice. What gives relief and comfort to one person, may do the opposite for another. I don't advocate any one therapy.*

Question: *Of all the mind-body medicine you tried, what helped you the most?*

Answer: *While I tried some different therapies, once or twice, the following are the therapies I decided to do regularly.*

1. Biofeedback: *to learn about tension and stress I was holding in my body. I had two sessions initially.*

2. Meditation: *ocean waves, guided verbal meditations, meditation music. I bought four CD's and rented others from the library every fortnight.*

3. Breathing: *for total body relaxation. I learned and then practiced this at home.*

4. Acupuncture: *with a Doctor of Chinese Medicine. I went once a week for four sessions, then every two weeks for the following month. After that, when I felt like it.*

5. Massage (acupressure): *Once a week, then every two weeks, then once a month.*

Question: *What is the upper cervical chiropractic technique for Meniere's disease?*

Answer: *This is a treatment to correct vertebra in the spine. Vertebra that have become misaligned through traumatic injury, such as a motor vehicle crash. The theory is once these misalignments are treated, the body can function optimally, and self-heal. People ask me about this, but I avoid any neck manipulations. Consequentially, I have no experiential information on this technique.*

Question: *What one piece of advice would you give regarding alternative therapies?*

Answer: *Many natural therapists I spoke with stressed one point: avoid any neck manipulations, so I stuck to that. Even when having sports massages, I asked therapists to leave the neck area alone. Also, be selective, use your powers of deduction and analysis. Research the pros and cons of the practices you may be considering.*

Question: *Did you have massage therapy?*

Answer: *Yes, but not just before or just after an attack! During remission times, massage can help increase circulation, reduce fluid build-up, relaxation, and stress relief, collectively contributing to reduces attacks.*

Question: *What is cranial-sacral therapy?*

Answer: *The therapy involves the re-balancing of the craniosacral system, through gentle non-invasive manipulation of the skull, and the bones of the face, and spine.*

Question: *What is osteopathy therapy?*

Answer: *Osteopathy treatment (OT) may be a positive complementary medicine for the four defining symptoms of Meniere's; by improving the function of abnormal tissues in the head, cervical, thoracic, and TMJ areas and provide symptomatic relief. Chiropractors or osteopaths may adjust the* head, jaw, and neck to relieve movement restrictions that could affect the inner ear. People have asked me about this therapy, but it was not part of my management plan.

Question: *What is kinesiology?*

Answer: *Applied kinesiology (AK) uses muscle strength testing to identify nutritional deficiencies and health problems. Weakness in certain muscles corresponds to specific diseases or body imbalances. Research suggests that Meniere's vertigo may improve with rotational exercises. However, this is still in the early stages of research, and it is not a common alternative therapy as yet.*

Question: *What is cranial osteopathy?*

Answer: *Craniosacral therapists use their hands to gently move the bones of the skull to relieve pressure on the head, which helps the nervous system function better.*

Question: *Can acupuncture help Meniere's disease symptoms?*

Answer: *The World Health Organization (WHO) lists Meniere's disease as one of 104 conditions that are treated with acupuncture. There are specific acupuncture points for ears, kidneys, sympathetic nervous system, and adrenal, which may help relieve dizziness associated with Meniere's disease.*

Question: *Did you try acupuncture?*

Answer: *Yes. It did help. After every session with a registered practitioner, I always felt better.*

Question: *Can acupressure massage help with symptoms?*

Answer: *Acupressure massage works on restoring the flow of energy within your body. Acupressure helped my extreme tiredness.*

Question: *Can Reiki help Meniere symptoms?*

Answer: *Reiki uses a technique commonly referred to as palm healing or hands-on healing. According to practitioners, the healing effects are mediated by channeling the universal energy known as Qi (pronounced 'chi'). This energy permeates our bodies but is not measurable by modern scientific techniques. It is thought to help relaxation, assist in the body's natural healing processes, and develop emotional, mental, and spiritual wellbeing. I liked this therapy.*

Question: *Can reflexology help Meniere symptoms?*

Answer: *Reflexology is reported to help treat symptoms of vertigo by restoring your body to a balanced energy flow. It works on a specific set of pressure points located in various parts of the body: cervical spine, ear, neck, hands, and feet.*

Question: *Are there any alternative treatments or remedies that can help relieve tinnitus symptoms?*

Answer: *Ginkgo may help relieve tinnitus in some people. Fenugreek tea (steeped in cold water) is known to stop cricket noises and ringing in the ears. Chamomile tea promotes relaxation and helps with sleep. Relaxation techniques can be beneficial: biofeedback, yoga, massage, and meditation of all kinds.*

Question: *Can Sea-Bands help nausea?*

Answer: *Yes, they can help sometimes. Sea-Bands are two small stretchy bands made of thick knitted fabric and a small plastic marble. Place one on each wrist, and the ball applies pressure to the acupressure points on the wrists.*

Question: *Did you take any homeopathic treatments?*

Answer: *Yes. I used homeopathy a lot as part of my self-help program. Homeopathy helps with anxiety and depression. I used Arnica drops taken in a small glass of water, after a Meniere's vertigo attack, to reduce stress.*

Question: *Did you use Bach Flower remedies?*

Answer: *I used a remedy called Rescue Remedy after a vertigo attack. I found that helped give me some bounce back and took some of the stress away after vertigo attacks.*

Question: *What specific aromatherapy oils did you use?*

Answer: *I used a variety such as Clary Sage, Tangerine, Sweet Orange, Sweet Basil or Holy Basil, Frankincense or Sacred Frankincense, mainly a few drops in the bath as bath oils. Some I burned in oil burners for the general atmosphere.*

Question: *Is the quality of aromatherapy oil important?*

Answer: *They must be pure essential oils with no additives from a reputable company. I used oils from The Tisserand Institute in The United Kingdom. They offer educational material of essential oils, and their safe usage, based on genuine evidence, scientific data, and credible research.*

Question: *How did you use essential oils?*

Answer: *I added six drops of selected oil into a warm bath. I used oils in a diffuser or an essential oil burner in the living room, and bedroom. Oils are for external use only and must be diluted in a carrier oil, such as almond oil, never use directly on the skin.*

Question: *What aromatherapy oils helped with vertigo?*

Answer: *While I can't say categorically that aromatherapy oils did or didn't help with vertigo, they did help me feel calmer and relaxed at home. They added a degree of comfort and a sense of wellbeing.*

Question: *What is ginger oil helpful for?*

Answer: *Ginger is used for nausea, also for relieving dizziness and vertigo, by increasing circulation to the brain.*

Question: *What is lavender oil helpful for?*

Answer: *Lavender is commonly used for relief of stress, anxiety, and depression, and is useful for dizziness.*

Question: *Is peppermint good for vertigo relief?*

Answer: *Peppermint is highly effective for dizziness and nausea. Rose is effective for depression and relaxation.*

Question: *What is rosemary oil helpful for?*

Answer: *Rosemary essential oil helps relieve depression, fatigue, and dizziness.*

ANSWERS FOR GETTING BETTER

Question: *What motivated you towards recovery? Can you give an example?*

Answer: *I had a week of vertigo attacks. When I managed to get myself up, I went and sat for a long time in the garden under the proverbial old apple tree, with its rope swing for the kids; the tree needed a prune, and a spray, its trunk covered with lichen, yet it was full of apple blossom, with bees buzzing. My young daughter came home from school and asked me to push her on the swing. I found the simple act of anticipating the rise and fall of the swing very demanding. I realized those simple pleasures were almost beyond me. That was a turning point when I decided to take responsibility for my recovery.*

Question: *Who encouraged you to make a full recovery?*

Answer: *I encouraged myself. I created strategies and set goals that I could achieve. My family was always there to support me in what I was doing.*

Question: *Do you have to be proactive for a recovery?*

Answer: *There is growing evidence to suggest that prompt treatment can help prevent the progression of a more chronic long-term condition. In my case, I established my recovery program within the first three months. I consider this development a major factor in my full recovery.*

Question: *Why was accepting you're condition vital to you?*

Answer: *Accepting and embracing a healthy coexistence with Meniere's was part of the cure. Coexistence for came from discovering possible causes for my Meniere's. Once I found ways to live with Meniere's, I was able to overcome it.*

Question: *When did you decide to not wallow in Meniere's?*

Answer: *The swing with my daughter was the turning point that snapped me out of the Meniere doldrums.*

Question: *Did you develop a personal philosophy?*

Answer: *My philosophy was the mantra: 'I will get better.'*

Question: *How did you go about recovering?*

Answer: *To be honest, when you feel bad, it's hard to find any space to do anything. It all seems too complicated. However, I had to start somewhere because I couldn't wait until I felt better. I started a simple, achievable self-help management plan to improve my health, which included meditation, diet, walking, and supplements. I also understood it couldn't be a static plan. It had to be a stepping stone strategy; achieve one goal and step to the next.*

Question: *What was the first goal?*

Answer: *My first goal was to walk two lamp-posts. Then four, then around the block. I achieved this over two weeks. A simple act, but it put me in control. The more I achieved, the more I overcame the dominance of Meniere's.*

Question: *What do you think made a difference?*

Answer: *Creating a manageable recovery program.*

Question: *Was getting better an easy thing to do?*

Answer: *No. It wasn't easy or fast. I used the three P's: Patience, Perseverance, and Persistence.*

Question: *If you were to sum up your philosophy, for recovery, what would it be?*

Answer: *Simple sense. I'd say making a recovery involved doing a lot of seemingly simple things. We tend to overlook the essential things these days, such as, resting, exercising, and enjoying nature. Nowadays, we can pop a tablet to calm down or sleep, disguise a headache or flu, but at what cost to overall health? The management techniques were simple.*

Question: *What were the best resolutions for Meniere's?*

Answer: *Not to get lost in the symptoms of the disease. Not to let Meniere's define me as a person. To believe that if I could reduce and eliminate the symptoms, I would get my life back, which turned out to be true.*

Question: *What were the five most significant purchases you made to help you with Meniere's?*

Answer:

1: *The monthly gym membership.*

2: *Walking shoes.*

3: *Noise blocker for noise recruitment.*

4: *Creating my low-salt cookbooks.*

5: *Windsurfers for my daughter and myself.*

Question: *How did you exercise your mind?*

Answer: *Reading books, listening to music, watching documentaries, spending time in the kitchen, travel, painting, writing, and learning new skills.*

Question: *Did Meniere's make you laid back or intense?*

Answer: *Laid-back was not my personality, but when I suffered Meniere's, I was forced onto my back. Now people say I am laid-back. I think that's good!*

Question: *How many hours did you work on the computer before Meniere's?*

Answer: *When I first sat at the computer, I suffered from an attack after twenty minutes. I tried again and the same thing happened. After that, I had to keep away from using computers for about a year and a half.*

Question: *How long was it before you could spend time on te computer?*

Answer: *After eighteen months, I managed fifteen minutes and then gradually worked my way up to half an hour. After an hour, I had to take a break then go back to half-hour periods of time.*

Question: *What effect did the computer have?*

Answer: *The brightness of the screen and the vertical scrolling movement was enough to trigger a Meniere's attack. I also found the computer made me tired.*

Question: *What do you say to other sufferers with regard to the computer?*

Answer: *If you are having a lot of vertigo attacks. Take a look at how much time you spend on the computer without taking a break. You must take breaks.*

Question: *Is this book published as an e-book?*

Answer: *No. Finding answers is demanding enough. I don't want sufferers to spend hours on the computer reading through questions and answers.*

Question: *How long could you spend reading a book?*

Answer: *Initially, I could only read for twenty minutes to half an hour at a time. Activities involving eye movements were triggers for me.*

Question: *If you had to choose one book for sufferers, what book would it be and why?*

Answer: *'Full Catastrophe Living'. It helped me with day to day stress. This book is about using mindfulness to* improve health and healing. The author Jon Kabat-Zinn, runs a highly acclaimed stress reduction program at the University of Massachusetts Medical Centre. The program has helped thousands of people cope with stress, anxiety, pain, and illness. I read this book cover to cover many times.

Question: *Did you read any other of his books?*

Answer: *Yes. I read 'Wherever You Go, There You Are'.*

Question: *How did you plan for a good night's sleep?*

Answer: *A lack of sleep is a significant cause of stress. I would spend time relaxing before going to sleep and stop doing any mentally demanding tasks four hours before going to bed. I often had a warm bath.*

Question: *When sleeping, did you keep your head flat or raised?*

Answer: *I always used a couple of pillows.*

Question: *When you slept, did you prefer to be flat on your back, curled up on your side, or your stomach?*

Answer: *I preferred to sleep on my side.*

Question: *What position did you usually wake up in?*

Answer: *On my side.*

Question: *What did you do when you couldn't sleep at night? Did you count sheep? Or get up out of bed?*

Answer: *Lying in bed, not sleeping, created anxiety so I'd get out of bed and eat a banana for the potassium.*

Question: *Did it help to have animals around when you were in bed?*

Answer: *I liked animals around and found them a comfort.*

Question: *Did you feel you got enough sleep?*

Answer: *Yes, although I was always tired.*

Question: *What time would you wake up in the mornings?*

Answer: *I would wake up before the sparrows woke, I would check in on how I was feeling, and if things felt normal, I would go back to sleep and wake again about 8 am.*

Question: *Were mornings your worst time of day?*

Answer: *No. During the night, if I woke with a vertigo attack, the morning was a time for recovery.*

Question: *What did you do when you got out of bed?*

Answer: *I would have breakfast. I needed to fuel up as soon as possible after waking.*

Question: *What was your favorite place in the house?*

Answer: *The back veranda overlooking the garden. The arbor covered with drooping clusters of purple wisteria, in the heat of summer.*

Question: *Did you take rests during the day?*

Answer: *I certainly did. I planned a rest mid-morning and then mid-afternoon. This was me taking time out for myself.*

Question: *What do you recommend for meditation?*

Answer: *Kabat-Zinn's four-part home training course allowed me to achieve deep states of relaxation and a wonderful sense of wellbeing.*

Question: *Why did you produce a meditation CD?*

Answer: *When I suffered from Meniere symptoms, I regularly listened to a series of guided meditations. And I thought Meniere people would like to hear a guided meditation by a person who understood Meniere's.*

Question: *What was your Refresher Nap?*

Answer: *I would take a refresher nap after and often before an activity. I could nap for twenty minutes and feel refreshed. Any longer and I ran the risk of sleep inertia — that unpleasant groggy feeling that takes a long time to shake off. I avoided taking naps later than 4:00 pm because I found it disrupted regular sleep.*

Question: *If you spent one hour doing nothing, what did you do?*

Answer: *I'd sit in the sunshine overlooking the bay. I always found it relaxing to sit and observe the boats, bird life, sunsets, clouds, and weather patterns.*

Question: *What paradox or contradiction in life have you had to accept or embrace?*

Answer: *Laziness! Laziness is nothing more than the habit of resting before you get tired. Laziness works. It's a way to incorporate health benefits into your life. I always thought laziness was a bad habit, but now I don't. It's having a 'laissez-faire' attitude, which simply means let go, or leave it to itself.*

Question: *Did Meniere's make you a creature of habit?*

Answer: *I gave up habitual living that involved the cycle of stress. I constantly tried to find new paradigms with Meniere's. By default, I discovered healthy habits along the way.*

I also didn't let Meniere's reduce me to a limited life.

Question: *Did Meniere's create any idiosyncrasies?*

Answer: *In the early stages of Meniere's, I had to self-monitor my activities to see the connection between triggers, and attacks, effects of vitamins, diet, exercise, meditation, and stress. This made me egocentric.*

Question: *Did you plan your day, or did the day plan you?*

Answer: *Acute symptoms planned my day. I had no say. If I didn't have those days, I would plan my activities. If I didn't achieve everything I'd planned, I would shift the unfinished items to the following day. I then congratulated myself regardless of how much I accomplished. Prior to Meniere's, it was my habit to finish the day with all the goals completed.*

Question: *How important was it to set goals?*

Answer: *Researcher Edwin Locke found that individuals who set specific goals performed better than those who set general, easy goals. Goal setting is paramount. Belief can also act as a goal. Believe you will get better and you will.*

Question: *Why is learning to say No so important?*

Answer: *Learning to say 'No' reduced my level of stress. I stopped taking on additional responsibility. I practiced saying* phrases such as; 'I am sorry, but I can't commit to this at the moment.' 'Now is not a good time as I'm in the middle of something.' 'Why don't you ask me again at...' 'I'd love to do this, but.' Taking time for yourself is essential for reducing stress and Meniere symptoms.

Question: *When you felt unwell, did you keep on going?*

Answer: *A definite no. Often this simple act of not going and going averted a vertigo attack.*

Question: *What did you consider a good day?*

Answer: *No attacks and doing everything on my wellness list, without feeling exhausted.*

Question: *What did you consider a great day?*

Answer: *Feeling relaxed doing everything I planned to do without any sign of Meniere's. These were my 'windows' where I felt I was living my life to the full again. Sometimes a good day was followed by a bad day, but the longer I used my recovery program, the more good days I experienced.*

Question: *How did you react when you finally 'managed' your attacks?*

Answer: *It was a long period of time, so the reaction was anticipation and hope. I worked out there was a Beginning, Middle, and End to the attack, and then I structured a* *management strategy for each stage. Applying the strategy took away the anxiety and confusion of the attacks. Plus, using diet, exercise and mindfulness, attacks became less intense, and less frequent. It took time, but I started to feel more and more confident that the lack of devastating symptoms was going to be my future. Years after my recovery, I still feel thankful I was able to recover fully.*

Question: *What did Meniere's teach you?*

Answer: *The consequence of not taking care of myself with Meniere's, was ruthless. If I were tired or stressed or didn't eat or drink correctly, I would have a vertigo attack. To counter this, I stopped getting tired and stressed, watched my diet, exercised regularly, which, when combined, lessened the severity and amount of attacks plus my energy levels increased.*

Question: *What stressed you out most?*

Answer: *Initially, day to day demands and not being able to meet them.*

Question: *What advice can you give to relieve stress?*

Answer: *Avoid stressful situations and activities. Participate in physical activity and mindfulness meditation, which not only relax you, they metabolize anti-stress hormones.*

Question: *What other ideas are there for relieving stress?*

Answer: *Talk to someone about how you're feeling, this releases built-up tension. Plus, you can strengthen your nervous system with vitamin supplements.*

Question: *What did you do when you needed to relax?*

Answer: *I'd soak for a long time in a warm bath with aromatherapy oils.*

Question: *Did you often feel overwhelmed?*

Answer: *Yes. In the initial months.*

Question: *What did you do to re-establish confidence?*

Answer: *I focused on small achievable activities.*

Question: *What made you feel OK?*

Answer: *Simple things really: reading the morning paper at a café down the road, or taking the occasional fish and chips lunch (without salt) down to the local disused pier I used to fish from as a boy. Initially, it was nice just being able to get out and about. In good periods I loved windsurfing in a natural shallow sea estuary with my daughter. You could hear the gulls calling over the dunes while we skimmed over calm blue water together.*

Question: *Did Meniere's make you superstitious?*

Answer: *Not superstitious, I would say vigilant. Once I set myself the goal to get better, I constantly monitored my internal and external environment to see how it affected me. Some things may have looked a little superstitious, like looking at the clouds building up and saying, 'This could be trouble.' With bad weather approaching, barometric pressure made me feel woozy, which indicated a vertigo attack might develop.*

Question: *Did you believe you would ever get better?*

Answer: *In the beginning, I wondered if I would ever make a recovery from Meniere's. I thought Meniere's was the new normal. Most days felt hopeless. I couldn't believe this was happening to me. I dreaded the relentless attacks of vertigo. It was when I started to manage Meniere's that the sense of hopelessness changed for the better. Bad days with Meniere's will always test your strength. Keep believing you can and will get better. Belief accompanied by action is the law for success.*

Question: *To what extent do you think a person's attitude influence healing?*

Answer: *I believe in quantum physics: Get the right attitude, and healing is a certainty. You can influence the direction of your life.*

Question: *What's something you lost by having Meniere's?*

Answer: *The career I had built up and all that goes with years of hard work.*

Question: *What is something you found through Meniere's?*

Answer: *I found that I listened to my body. I became more aware of my actions and reactions. Self-awareness acted as my map back to a feeling of wellbeing.*

Question: *What is the worst thing a person without Meniere's said to you?*

Answer: *'Meniere's was a mere minor inconvenience.'*

Question: *What drove you crazy about Meniere's?*

Answer: *Not being in control. I lost confidence in the stability of my life.*

Question: *What has been the biggest challenge of Meniere's?*

Answer: *Not allowing Meniere's disease to take over my life and personality, but to work with it, to beat the symptoms. Getting that balance right helped me look after myself and move ahead towards recovery.*

Question: *What was your greatest life challenge?*

Answer: *Losing a successful career to Meniere's and reconfiguring my life from there.*

Question: *What do you think was your strongest attribute for recovery?*

Answer: *A positive attitude. In times of serious illness, you must hold a strong belief in a positive outcome, regardless of the hell you are going through at the time. It takes a positive attitude to keep a positive outlook. Positivity overall is what gives one the strength to overcome the disabling effects of Meniere's disease. A positive attitude is powerful medicine.*

Question: *What was something having a chronic disease changed about you?*

Answer: *My sense of certainty about the present and the future. The present is more important to me now. I also increased my wellness.*

Question: *What could Meniere's never change about you?*

Answer: *Positive attitude, the power of love and family. The belief that self-determination makes a difference to life.*

Question: *What do you never take for granted?*

Answer: *Appreciating good health. I feel privileged to have a second chance at doing life.*

Question: *What did you do in your free time?*

Answer: *This changed as the disease progressed. Initially, the list would be; sit on the sofa, rest, sit outside, walk, rest. Then later, many things were home-based, like doing fix-up jobs around the house, cooking, working in the garden, reading, watching TV, listening to music, walking, being a family guy. Then I added more sport activities like doing gym, fishing, and traveling. After my recovery, I was able to do everything I did before, except scuba.*

Question: *Does caffeine affect Meniere's?*

Answer: *Caffeine raises the body's blood volume and causes small blood vessels to constrict. This reduces the blood supply to the ear causing inner ear pressure and fullness. Because of its affect on the cerebral vascular system, coffee can increase tinnitus levels and is a trigger for causing Meniere attacks.*

Question: *Did you have to give up coffee?*

Answer: *I gave up my habitual strong caffeinated coffee, and switched to decaffeinated coffee.*

Question: *What was your favorite beverage?*

Answer: *Hot drinks like fresh lemon juice or lime with a teaspoon of honey in hot water, also, herbal teas. There are delicious tisanes available that use herbal teas combined with spices and fruit, such as green tea and ginger.*

Question: *Is there caffeine in medications?*

Answer: *Yes. Caffeine can be produced synthetically and added to medications. If you are cutting down your caffeine intake, be aware that some non-prescription drugs such as a headache and pain reliever tablets can contain 65 mg of caffeine per tablet. Product labels are required to list caffeine in the ingredients but not required to state the actual amount of the substance.*

Question: *Is there caffeine in certain foods and drinks?*

Answer: *Yes. It's not just coffee that contains caffeine. Black tea contains 40-70 mg of caffeine, and a 1.45 oz sweet chocolate bar contains 27 mg of caffeine. A small can of Red Bull contains 80 mg, a 12 oz Coca-Cola Classic has 34.5 mg of caffeine and Diet Coke has 46.5 mg, Pepsi-Cola 37.5 mg. You need to look at the ingredients panel on products.*

Question: *Do you drink coffee, now you are better?*

Answer: *Yes. I'd bought an Italian coffee machine made of solid brass with an eagle perched on top. The eagle sat there and lost its shine while waiting for the day when I would flick the red switch and fire him up. That day came. Now I'm* back enjoying lattes, flat whites, and espressos. Yes! Finally, the Italian, Brazilian, Columbian, and Arabica are back in my blood. I do limit them to a maximum of two cups of coffee a day.

Question: *Does alcohol affect Meniere disease?*

Answer: *Alcohol can cause the blood vessels to contract, which restricts the blood supply to your inner ear. Surprisingly though, small amounts of alcohol, such as a glass of red wine or half a pint of beer a day, can help peripheral circulation. In the early stages, I didn't drink any alcohol. Now my alcohol consumption is 2 or 3 glasses a week.*

Question: *Why should you cut down or avoid alcohol?*

Answer: *Alcohol affects both your balance and your vascular system. The more your drink, the less stable you feel, and the more your blood pressure will rise. Using alcohol as a way to alleviate stress is not helpful.*

Question: *Do you drink alcohol now you are better?*

Answer: *Yes, but always in moderation. For health, I don't go over the recommended daily units.*

Question: *What should you never feel guilty about?*

Answer: *Feeling lazy, taking breaks, and taking time out.*

Question: *Did Meniere's make you serious-minded, or did you keep your sense of humor?*

Answer: *They say laughter is the best medicine. Even on the worst days, I tried to keep my humor.*

Question: *How can humor help with Meniere's?*

Answer: *A good laugh goes a long way to having a happy life. When you are down, switch to the comedy channel and watch comedy programs.*

Question: *What was something that brought a smile to your face?*

Answer: *I loved watching laugh-out-loud comedy programs. It helped lighten up my attitude, and nothing seemed so bad. Humor, whether an in-house joke or seeing the funny side, picked me up whenever I was feeling down.*

Question: *Do you believe staying positive helped in your recovery?*

Answer: *Yes. Once I was over the initial shock. I worked on maintaining a positive attitude by taking every effort to replace negative thoughts with positive ones.*

Question: *Did you watch movies?*

Answer: *Yes I did. I learned by trial and error never to sit in the front rows of the theatre. Surrounded by fast moving images was a trigger for an attack. I chose seating in the middle or back of the theatre with the screen directly in front of me.*

Question: *What is your favorite Meniere Man quote?*

Answer: *The more you do, the more you can do.*

Question: *Where was your favorite place to be?*

Answer: *At home. The home was a sanctuary for me on so many levels.*

Question: *What was your favorite season?*

Answer: *The summer season because the barometric levels were more settled and for the opportunity to get outside more.*

Question: *Does hot or cold weather affect symptoms?*

Answer: *Winter for sure. Storms brought low barometric pressure, which triggered attacks.*

Question: *What one thing did you wish for most?*

Answer: *To put Meniere's disease behind me.*

Question: *What t-shirt slogan would you write for Meniere's disease?*

Answer: *Breathe.*

Question: *Which of your five senses do you treasure most?*

Answer: *The sense of hearing as communication is vital for a social life. Meniere's made me profoundly deaf in my right ear, and then Exostoses (surfer's ear) caused deafness as well. Thankfully, I do have hearing aids that bring me back into the hearing world.*

Question: *If forced to give up one more of your senses, which one would it be?*

Answer: *You do realize when you lose an aspect of your senses, how important they are to feeling alive. I don't want to give up any more senses.*

Question: *What's something you regret losing most?*

Answer: *I regret losing the things I can never find again, like my hearing, I will never get that back again.*

Question: *What are the best sounds to your ears?*

Answer: *Birdsong and the ocean waves.*

Question: *What are the worst sounds?*

Answer: *Loud, sharp noises like firecrackers, sudden unexpected noises, and someone talking to me very quietly.*

Question: *Did you listen to music or prefer quiet?*

Answer: *I preferred quiet when I suffered from Meniere's.*

Question: *What are the lasting legacies of having had Meniere's disease?*

Answer: *Roaring tinnitus and deafness in the affected ear. The rush of fear when I feel dizzy.*

Question: *What was your greatest achievement with Meniere's?*

Answer: *Recovering fully, and helping others with this disease.*

Question: *What events in your life have brought about the greatest life-change?*

Answer: *Getting married and having children, I became a family man. Meniere's diagnosis, because that turned me into Meniere Man.*

Question: *What's your reaction to people who don't understand Meniere's?*

Answer: *My reaction to people without empathy or refuse to acknowledge the impact of Meniere's, is to stay away as far as possible. They will never take the time or care to understand. So it depends on who it is and what effect they have on you. I know one man who had all the information on the Meniere's, yet he still referred to Meniere's as a mere minor inconvenience. That man was instrumental in the ill fate of many people with Meniere's, myself included.*

Question: *What issues about Meniere's fire you up?*

Answer: *Lack of understanding by non-sufferers. Yes, even family and friends can be dismissive and expect one to just get over it, which is demeaning. Sufferers are vulnerable on a physical, mental, and emotional level, and they don't often receive the support necessary to cope. And worse, there are people in society who are aggressive predators, looking to take advantage of what they perceive as weakness. So be aware and seek as much genuine support as you can.*

Question: *What one thing is detrimental to recovery?*

Answer: *The bitter pill. Don't swallow the bitter pill. Don't harbor grudges, petty jealousies, or stress about everything, don't hold onto a negative attitude towards life and how life has treated you. Try to avoid the negative, whether a thought, word, or deed. In my experience, the more you let go of negativity, the more Meniere's lets go of you.*

Question: *What do you recommend to overcome self-pity?*

Answer: *'Act and act now.'*

Question: *If you could have changed anything about your Meniere's experience, what would it be?*

Answer: *I would have changed the lack of knowledge surrounding Meniere's.*

Question: *If you could have eliminated one symptom from Meniere's, what would it be?*

Answer: *The vertigo attacks. Then Meniere's would have been a mere minor inconvenience.*

Question: *If you had been assured you would get better, what would you have attempted?*

Answer: *I would have kept my career going by taking an extended leave of absence and coming back to work when I could.*

Question: *If you could change one thing about your Meniere's experience, what would that be?*

Answer: *To be diagnosed more in the future, when there was a lot more information, and research available.*

Question: *If you could give a gift to a fellow sufferer, what would that be?*

Answer: *The gift of a complete recovery.*

Question: *If you could cure a disease, what would it be?*

Answer: *Alzheimer's disease.*

Question: *What advice would you give sufferers?*

Answer: *The more you do, the better you feel. The better you feel, the more you achieve.*

Question: *If you had Meniere's over again, what would you do differently?*

Answer: *I would seek as much advice as possible before I made any major decisions.*

Question: *Was your illness a season of life, or part of life?*

Answer: *Meniere's was the winter of my life.*

Question: *What residual reminders do you have?*

Answer: *Deafness in one ear and tinnitus. On my life path, the loss of my career.*

Question: *If you could hang a motto in every sufferer's home, what would it say?*

Answer: *The more you do, the more you can do.*

Question: *If you had five pieces of advice to pass on to sufferers, what would it be?*

Answer: *The first: Don't be tempted to rush into cures. The second: Don't try to 'quick fix' with surgery. The third: Realize there is a lot you can do to help yourself get over Meniere's. The fourth: Practice patience. It can take some time to make a recovery, it doesn't happen overnight, but it does happen. The fifth: Don't give up hope.*

Question: *What advice can you give to conquer fear?*

Answer: *Fear comes from the unknown. Get the facts, get answers to your questions — voice your fears. Talk to people you trust. Knowledge and emotional support helps dissipate fear.*

Question: *What is the one personal attribute that you believe is essential for recovery?*

Answer: *Determination to achieve the goal of recovery.*

Question: *What does health mean to you now?*

Answer: *True success in life.*

Question: How would you define good health?

Answer: Health is a state of complete physical, mental, and social wellbeing.

Question: What is more important, health or wealth?

Answer: At one stage in my life, I thought money was most important. I didn't pay that much attention to health. I left health to take care of itself. Having been through Meniere's, I'd say health is the real wealth.

Question: What is your thought on conquering Meniere's?

Answer: Don't accept what you cannot control.

Question: What thing do you know about Meniere's that you are certain of.

Answer: Prosper Meniere discovered the disease.

Question: Was Meniere's the most severe illness you've had to face?

Answer: Yes, so far in my life, it has been. If I ever find myself with another serious disease or illness, I will apply the same self-help principles as I did for Meniere's.

Question: *How different are you now, than before?*

Answer: *I have greater respect for how I think. Meniere's showed me how powerful the mind is, for healing.*

Question: *What personal habits did you break?*

Answer: *The habit of multitasking to excess. I stopped stacking one activity on another, all day, every day.*

Question: *Was Meniere's a traumatic event?*

Answer: *Yes, it was a life-changing event.*

Question: *What character trait did Meniere's change?*

Answer: *I learned to say NO without feeling guilty.*

Question: *Was there ever a time when you thought you would die?*

Answer: *No, never. Although there were days when I almost wished I could!*

Question: *What was the hardest era of your life?*

Answer: *My time negotiating the mountain of Meniere. I stumbled on all of its stones. It was an uphill battle and a test of personal endurance and strength at times.*

Question: *What do you think was a Meniere's epiphany?*

Answer: *Seeing the connection between triggers and attacks. Understanding that relationship was the turning point. I armed myself with personal facts to begin to counter the vertigo attacks.*

Question: *Before Meniere's was your glass half empty or half full?*

Answer: *It was half full, for sure.*

Question: *What was your most significant loss?*

Answer: *A feeling of confidence and as the French say, joie de vivre. The enjoyment of everything in life was difficult because symptoms have a way of stealing happiness.*

Question: *Why do you think you had Meniere's?*

Answer: *I think I developed Meniere's, due to a long period of high stress.*

Question: *With Meniere's, did you feel like you were merely existing or living?*

Answer: *In the beginning, Meniere's dominated my every waking hour. I felt like a shadow of myself, and I merely existed. Later, once I had taken control, I felt I was living life again.*

Question: *How did you make peace with yourself?*

Answer: *Acceptance. This was the key. I stopped fighting Meniere's and accepted the disease. Accepting the condition lead to my recovery.*

Question: *Meniere's is a cathartic experience. How did that fuel impetus?*

Answer: *To overcome a major personal hurdle like Meniere's opens possibilities. That has stayed with me, and now I feel confident and excited to try the seemingly impossible.*

Question: *What lessons did illness teach you?*

Answer: *Good old-fashioned moderation and discipline. Also, to truly listen to my body and pay attention to intuition.*

Question: *Diagnosed all over again, what would you do?*

Answer: *I would start Meniere management on day one. I wouldn't waste a day. There is a lot you can do to help yourself. Focus on getting your body healthy. Make proactive lifestyle changes; exercise, diet, supplements, and stress relief. No matter what Meniere's throws at you, strive to keep a positive attitude.*

Question: *What did you manage to achieve through your long journey with Meniere's disease?*

Answer: *I managed to understand my Meniere's. Then I worked out how to cope with symptoms and get better.*

Question: *What positives have resulted from your experience with Meniere's?*

Answer: *The virtual elimination of everything that appeared negative or harmful to me, both emotionally and physically.*

Question: *How do you comfort someone who is suffering from Meniere's?*

Answer: *Trust your body to get better.*

Question: *How is life after Meniere's for you?*

Answer: *Life with Meniere's and life without Meniere's are poles apart. Once I recovered from Meniere's, I felt like I had my life back again. Now, I'm not only well, but I also snowboard, surf, hike, travel, and work on my computer for hours. In short, I live a full and active life. If you saw me a few years ago... I struggled to get out of bed.*

Question: *Do you have a 'bucket list?'*

Answer: *Don't we all? Suffering from Meniere's took a chunk of time away from me. My calendar is full, and I'm not wasting a day of it.*

Question: *Why is getting out and about important?*

Answer: *Getting out and about allows you to be part of society and to feel normal. Not going out, puts sufferers at risk of isolation, loneliness, and depression.*

Question: *Did you ever have an attack while driving?*

Answer: *No. I never had an attack while driving a car. I took control of the car only when I felt capable. If your condition makes it difficult to operate a vehicle for a while, consider transportation alternatives such as public transport or getting out with a friend at the wheel.*

Question: *Did you plan your vacations?*

Answer: *Vacations were planned in detail to avoid stress and fatigue.*

Question: *Can you go on a boat with Meniere's?*

Answer: *Yes, you can go sailing, or go on a cruise. If you get seasick in rough weather, you won't be alone. In fact, your balance system may well benefit from a little rocking and rolling. I often went sailing and fishing in small craft. Rocking on the ocean wasn't a trigger for me. However, if I were having a series of bad days, then I wouldn't go.*

Question: *Could you travel by train with Meniere's?*

Answer: *Yes, I could travel by train with Meniere's. A word of advice: don't try and follow the fast moving scene outside the window. Read a book.*

Question: *How did you cope with air travel?*

Answer: *To help prevent fatigue, I avoided purchasing tickets on red-eye flights. I booked daytime flights, chose routes with the least time zone changes, and included stopovers, to let my body catch up. I'd book an aisle seat away from service areas, in the forward section of the aircraft for better airflow. I would also book a seat over the wings for less movement during turbulence. I used earplugs and eyeshades to cut out light and noise. I pre-ordered low salt meals, stayed hydrated, and avoided alcohol. Travel for a Meniere sufferer is all about self-preservation and planning. The airplane is the last place you want a vertigo attack.*

Question: *Did flying cause you ear pain?*

Answer: *I made long-haul plane trips and never once suffered ear pain. I was initially apprehensive thinking about how the pressure in the plane would affect my Meniere's. Then I realized, cabin pressure affects the middle ear, not the inner ear. So I need not have worried on that account.*

Question: *What are your five essential tips for travel?*

Answer:

1: *Avoid getting overtired.*

2: *Keep sight of your dietary requirements.*

3: *Avoid stress.*

4: *Make the most of your vacation time.*

5: *Enjoy yourself!*

Question: *What was your most memorable travel experience with Meniere's?*

Answer: *Traveling with the family to the mountains and being Meniere free where I was vertigo free, for two weeks.*

Question: *What is something you did with Meniere's that surprised you?*

Answer: *Arriving with family in Whistler after a four-hour car journey from Vancouver. My Canadian friend, Al, handed out pairs of cross-country skis for a one hour night time trek. If he had asked me beforehand, I would have said no. The moonlight trek was incredible, and we all loved it —quite a feat when I look back at it now. Proof you really can do more than you think.*

ANSWERS TO LIVING THE MENIERE'S LIFE

Question: *What happened in the months prior to getting Meniere's Disease?*

Answer: *I had a four-month battle with a water-borne parasite I had contracted in the tropics. The parasite required two courses of powerful antiviral medication. Shortly afterward, I had my first vertigo attack.*

Question: *How healthy or unhealthy were you when you got sick?*

Answer: *I had both healthy and unhealthy habits. I did gym regularly, was active in sports, walked, and ate a healthy diet. But I also worked a sixty-hour week, socialized, drank copious cups of coffee, and indulged in food and drink at regular late-night business occasions. Having a business and a young family occupied all my time. I didn't take time out for myself.*

However, there were signs I was on the verge of exhaustion. I just accepted that was the way of it.

Question: *Did you blame your habits for making you sick?*

Answer: *Living a high-stress business life was a major suspicion for why I was ill.*

Question: *Do you think you need to set boundaries for good health?*

Answer: *Most definitely. Boundaries also need to adapt to your age. At forty-five, you need to work smarter, not harder.*

Question: *Describe your Meniere's disease onset?*

Answer: *Everyone seems to remember in detail the first attack of vertigo. I was staying in a hotel opposite the Grand Opera House in Paris. However, no amount of opulent surroundings could rid me of the horrible spinning bout I was experiencing. I couldn't figure out what was causing me to feel so ill. I put it down to food poisoning from lunch. I realize now, it was my first Meniere's vertigo attack.*

Question: *How old were you when diagnosed?*

Answer: *Meniere's disease arrived just after my forty-sixth birthday.*

Question: *How did you feel your age?*

Answer: *I felt I was too young to be diagnosed with an incurable disease.*

Question: *What were your frightening Meniere moments?*

Answer: *My first attack of vertigo in a business meeting. Hearing a car alarm going off in the driveway and being told there was no alarm. Later I learned it was the spontaneous onset of tinnitus.*

Question: *What did the diagnosis mean to you?*

Answer: *It was incomprehensible to me, and initially left me in a state of numbness and confusion.*

Question: *How did you feel when you were diagnosed?*

Answer: *It was one of the worst days of my life. I wasn't expecting to be diagnosed with anything. I just thought I had an ear infection. I had never heard of Meniere's disease. I couldn't understand why I had this Meniere's. I was the owner of a company, and I was married with a young family of two. The diagnosis gave me a terrible feeling of pending consequences for my family and business life.*

Question: *In five words, how would you sum up your Meniere's diagnosis?*

Answer: *Confusion. Shock. Fear. Loss. Trepidation.*

Question: *Did a Meniere's diagnosis leave you with regret, shame, or guilt?*

Answer: *Yes, all three, I regretted that I hadn't taken more care of myself. Guilt about not being able to control and stabilize my home and financial life. Shame about having a disease.*

Question: *Was there ever a time when your blood ran cold?*

Answer: *It had to be when the doctor slapped on that label of an incurable chronic condition called Meniere's.*

Question: *What comes to mind with the word vertigo?*

Answer: *A vortex of spinning into hyperspace.*

Question: *What was the prognosis for Meniere disease?*

Answer: *The ENT specialist told me I would have Meniere's for life. He added that there was no cure for it. Keep away from salt and stress.*

Question: *How sad did Meniere's make you feel?*

Answer: *I was extremely upset about the fact that my life was revolving around Meniere attacks. I would wake up thinking about Meniere's, spend the day thinking about Meniere's, and go to sleep worrying about Meniere's. It wasn't like anything I had encountered before, like a bad flu, when after a couple of weeks, you recover. The Meniere experience was all-consuming initially, but when I put my self-help regime in place, I gained control and a sense of hope.*

Question: *What was your idea of a bad day?*

Answer: *A vertigo attack with associated vomiting.*

Question: *Did you get warning signs for an attack?*

Answer: *Yes. I would feel strangely exhausted, a feeling of being dog tired even if I hadn't been doing much to warrant that kind of tiredness. At the same time, my hearing would drop, and I would have trouble hearing what people were saying; a sensation of cotton wool compacted in my ears made sound muffled. Tinnitus picked up and seemed louder. Wooziness increased.*

Question: *What would you do when you had a Meniere's vertigo attack?*

Answer: *I would lie on my back without moving my head a millimeter. Any movement to left or right increased the spinning dramatically.*

Question: *What did you think about when lying in bed?*

Answer: *Every time I turned over, I thought it might end in vertigo. I had difficulty trying not to think about worrying thoughts. I found the best idea was no thought.*

Question: *What did you think about when you were having an acute attack of vertigo?*

Answer: *At first I was frightened, later I used and repeated a thought from my mindful recovery strategy, 'This will end, I will get better.'*

Question: *How intense can vertigo attacks be?*

Answer: *Attacks are severe. There is no other experience I can compare with Meniere's vertigo. Rotational spinning for an hour is an experience a non-sufferer could ever understand.*

Question: *How many days in a month could you expect to experience vertigo?*

Answer: *The worst I recorded was a series of twelve attacks over a month.*

Question: *How often did you get vertigo?*

Answer: *The first year was the worst. I experienced attacks and associated recovery roughly three or four times a month.*

Question: *Did you ever go to the emergency room?*

Answer: *No. Luckily the doctor did house calls, and twice, he came and administered stematol by injection.*

Question: *Who gave you the most support?*

Answer: *Definitely my partner. She was amazing.*

Question: *In an emergency, who did you call?*

Answer: *I would tell my partner. She understood my plight. She also planned, organized, researched, and did a lot to make my time with Meniere's less complicated.*

Question: *Did Meniere's give you panic attacks?*

Answer: *Yes. At the slightest sensation of dizziness, I'd have a rush of anxiety; heart racing and cold sweats. Meniere attack anxiety happened for a year until I developed my Meniere recovery plan. Then anxiety lessened considerably.*

Question: *Meniere's brings uncertainty. How did you cope?*

Answer: *Meniere's certainly brings uncertainty. As well as trying to cope with vertigo attacks, the loss of life's equilibrium gave me an increasing worry about where Meniere's disease was taking my family, and myself. However, I endeavored to sustain faith and hope for a better outcome. I also* instigated a management plan for coping with Meniere's with the end objective of getting better. All of this helped with the uncertainty.

Question: *Did Meniere's affect your sense of wellbeing?*

Answer: *Yes definitely, for the first time in my life, I felt a constant sense of anxiety and fear. The specialists and doctors had no definitive answers to manage the condition. Not knowing what to do was a ground zero experience.*

Question: *What was your usual mood?*

Answer: *In the early days, I was in a preoccupied rather indecisive state, all due to the uncertainty of vertigo attacks.*

Question: *Did Meniere's make you feel alone?*

Answer: *Often, very alone. Support groups were non-existent. Had there been support groups, I would have had an easier time coping at the onset of the disease.*

Question: *Did you ever feel like a slave to Meniere's disease?*

Answer: *In the beginning, Meniere's enslaved my life. But the more I understood about triggers and my feelings, the more control I gained. Then I was able to predict and avoid an attack, or lessen its intensity. Also, understanding the mechanism of the vertigo attack helped. I was able to apply a management* plan to the vertigo attack that was identified as the Beginning, Middle, and End (BME) of the attack. The BME made a tremendous difference in reducing the vertigo effect of Meniere's.

Question: *What were the lows of Meniere's?*

Answer: *The acute attacks of vertigo. For a long while, I felt like they were breaking my spirit.*

Question: *What did you do when you felt overburdened by Meniere's Disease?*

Answer: *I fixed easy things around the home, like put new screws into a lock. Also, I sat in the sun, or went for a walk.*

Question: *Did confrontation with others affect you?*

Answer: *Most definitely. The confrontation aspect with people was one of the worst things for me. Emotional blowouts, by their stressful nature, can put you in the vertigo attack zone. I learned to pick my battles and not sweat as much small stuff. To let things be.*

Question: *Could you argue with your partner?*

Answer: *I made every effort to avoid conflict, however, as you know, this isn't always possible. I also think partners need to cut the Meniere sufferer some slack and avoid .stress.*

Question: *How did you keep the peace?*

Answer: *I tried not to sweat the small stuff. I read the book, 'Don't Sweat The Small Stuff' by Richard Carlson. Arguments were never worth the stress at the time or the fallout afterward. I meditated, attempted to be more positive, and see the bigger picture. I used to be able to see the big picture, but small things started to get to me, more and more.*

Question: *When you found yourself in a stressful situation, what did you do?*

Answer: *I walked away, to talk another day.*

Question: *Did arguments cause Meniere vertigo attacks?*

Answer: *I can't say for sure, but after an argument, I would invariably have an attack in the days following. I advocate avoiding stress.*

Question: *Did you feel angry at times?*

Answer: *I became more prone to mild anger outbursts. The anger outbursts were mainly due to frustration.*

Question: *How did you deal with anger?*

Answer: *Actively pursuing my goal of recovery, was my antidote to anger.*

Question: *What things made you feel depressed sometimes?*

Answer: *Not being able to function at my previous level, in everything.*

Question: *Did you secretly long to be rescued?*

Answer: *Yes, I wished there was a mentor for Meniere's. Someone to show me the pitfalls and opportunities. I wanted my ENT specialist to rescue me, but he truthfully said there was no long term answer.*

Question: *What was missing in your life with Meniere's?*

Answer: *Freedom to do what I wanted, without having to factor in Meniere's.*

Question: *What part of Meniere's had the most significant impact on you?*

Answer: *Spontaneous attacks take away social confidence, and spinning vertigo takes away planetary stability, leaving one constantly uncertain.*

Question: *What fears did you have to overcome?*

Answer: *The fear of never getting a happy, positive life back.*

Question: *Did you ever seek counseling?*

Answer: *I did. I felt such an overwhelming personal struggle with the loss of career and health at the same time. Unchecked grief, guilt, and shame made me begin to feel worthless, inadequate, and insignificant. I had to do something, so on the recommendation of my doctor, I went to a psychologist. He helped me cope with loss and grief.*

Question: *Do you think there is a certain amount of denial?*

Answer: *If you're in denial, you're trying to protect yourself by refusing to accept the truth about something that's happening in your life. To some degree, initial short-term denial can be a good thing. It can provide you with time to adjust and to look at the possibility of a life change. Denial has a dark side, it can prevent you from dealing with issues that require action, and those same issues left too long, can add to the problem.*

Question: *Did you live in denial at all?*

Answer: *For sure. As an active man, I found the diagnosis almost impossible to accept, and I was embarrassed to admit my disease. I pretend everything was normal, nothing wrong. Then I thought things like...the specialist is wrong; I don't have Meniere's.*

Question: *Did denial make things better or worse?*

Answer: *For me, denial only made things worse. I kept trying to work and run family life ar my usual pace, but it made the attacks worse.*

Question: *How long were you in denial?*

Answer: *At least three months! I tried to ignore the fact that Meniere's was going to change my life significantly. I kept going with my habits of drinking coffee and working long hours. But as symptoms got worse, I altered those patterns.*

Question: *How long until you accepted you had Meniere's?*

Answer: *I began to accept Meniere's being part of my life, after twelve months. That point was the beginning of my journey towards getting better. Every ending creates a new beginning, as long as you know, when one journey ends and the other begins.*

ON THE QUESTION OF MENIERE'S HEARING

Question: *What is aural fullness?*

Answer: *A feeling of pressure, discomfort, and a fullness sensation in the ears. It feels like your ear is plugged with cotton wool; sounds you hear become unclear, and distant.*

Question: *What causes aural fullness in the ears?*

Answer: *Episodic fluctuating aural fullness is due to the build-up of pressure in the inner ear, and often associated with the onset of an attack.*

Question: *Can you go deaf from Meniere's disease?*

Answer: *Yes. If you have unilateral Meniere's, the affected ear will lose some degree of hearing. There are varying levels of deafness found in the affected ear of people with Meniere's.*

If you have bilateral Meniere's you will likely have extreme difficulty with your hearing, but hearing professionals can help with this.

Question: *Why does Meniere's disease cause deafness?*

Answer: *The hearing loss is due to a sensorineural type of nerve deafness. During an attack, the cochlear hair cells of the inner ear become bathed in sodium and potassium, due to the sudden rupturing of the Reissner membrane. This rupturing occurs every time you have an attack. These hair cells are responsible for transmitting sound impulses to the brain. As they become damaged, so does your hearing facility in the affected ear.*

Question: *Does Meniere's disease cause conductive hearing loss?*

Answer: *No, conductive hearing loss happens when there is a problem in the middle ear. Meniere's hearing loss is the inner ear.*

Question: *Can you get high-frequency hearing loss?*

Answer: *Typically, the hearing loss in Meniere's is in the lower frequencies, associated with levels required for listening to speech.*

Question: *What is Meniere's unilateral hearing loss?*

Answer: *Hearing loss in one ear, the affected ear.*

Question: *What is a sensorineural hearing loss?*

Answer: *Sensorineural hearing loss has its origins in the inner ear (the sensory hearing organ). It also includes damage to the neural pathways of hearing (nerves).*

Question: *Is hearing loss permanent with Meniere's disease?*

Answer: *The intensity and range of hearing deterioration caused by Meniere's are different for everyone. But once Meniere's is advanced, your level of hearing loss becomes permanent.*

Question: *What is the permanent hearing damage?*

Answer: *Most people sustain moderate to severe hearing loss in the affected ear within three to seven years of diagnosis.*

Question: *Can Meniere's disease hearing loss be prevented?*

Answer: *Unfortunately, there is no known way to prevent the natural progression of hearing loss. It is vital to protect the hearing you have by protecting your ears against power tools or listening to loud music with headphones.*

Question: *Is hearing loss the same for everyone?*

Answer: *No. Hearing loss varies from person to person.*

I lost hearing rapidly and soon became ninety percent deaf in the affected ear; other people I spoke to told me they lost hearing slowly, and some never become deaf in the affected ear.

Question: *Can you have Meniere's without hearing loss?*

Answer: *It's part of the condition to lose part of your hearing permanently. Most Meniere sufferers experience permanent hearing loss to some degree.*

Question: *What is the difference between Meniere's and BPPV?*

Answer: *Within the inner ear is a structure called the labyrinth with semicircular canals, which hold fluids that help monitor the position and rotation of your head. Benign Paroxysmal Positional Vertigo (BPPV) is vertigo, which occurs with movements of the head such as lying down, turning over in bed, turning the head. The difference between BPPV and Meniere's disease is that Meniere's vertigo is not related to head position.*

Question: *What are crystals in the ear?*

Answer: *The balance system in the inner ear has otolith organs that contain tiny crystals. These crystals can become dislodged for no known reason and float into the semicircular canals. When this happens, this can cause intense dizziness and a spinning sensation that lasts less than five minutes. These symptoms collectively are called Paroxysmal Positional Vertigo.*

Question: *Does the Epley maneuver work for Meniere's?*

Answer: *Epley works to help relieve vertigo symptoms in BPPV. However, Meniere's is sensorineural, not crystal related.*

Question: *Can you have Meniere's disease and otosclerosis?*

Answer: *Yes, you certainly can. Otosclerosis prevents sound from passing through to the inner ear due to the stiffening of small bones (ossicles) in the ear canal. And you can get it in either ear. I had Meniere's disease in one ear and later diagnosed with otosclerosis in the other. The ENT specialist said it was 'Murphy's law,' meaning I was just plain unlucky to have otosclerosis in my good ear.*

Question: *Why do normal sounds appear incredibly loud?*

Answer: *This is due to hyperacusis: a hypersensitivity to normal sounds. The ear loses its ability to cope with quick shifts in sound levels.*

Question: *How did loud noises affect you?*

Answer: *Yes. There are two things the human body never adapts to; sudden noises and vertigo. The body will adapt to most other sensory changes but never to those two. Consequently, sound is listed by psychologists as psychological stress.*

Question: *What did you do to cope with loud sounds?*

Answer: *As I experienced more hearing loss, I found that normal environmental sounds appeared unbearably loud, even sounds like someone shutting a window. So I had to tell my family and friends when the environments were too loud for me. We'd move to a quiet corner or go outside. I also used a protective hearing device; a custom made sound diffuser like musicians wear during live concerts. Soft foam earplugs for hearing protection, purchased from a drug store or chemist, also work well for this.*

Question: *Describe the recruitment phenomenon in Meniere's disease?*

Answer: *Another reason why normal sounds may be unbearable is the recruitment factor associated with hearing loss; this is an abnormal increase in the perception of loudness, even though the noise may be slight. Have you noticed the recruitment factor in a café? You're quietly sipping a decaffeinated latte, and suddenly, the waitress drops a stainless spoon onto the tile floor; you get a super-shock! That's the recruitment factor.*

Question: *Can you experience ear pain?*

Answer: *Yes, you can. Although ear pain is not a symptom of Meniere's disease, aural fullness is. In some people, this fullness causes acute ear pain at times.*

Question: *Can Meniere's disease cause an ear infection?*

Answer: *No. Meniere's disease doesn't cause ear infections. Neither is Meniere's disease an ear infection. There can be a tendency to feel your ears are blocked up. Don't be tempted to dig the 'fullness' out with cotton buds!*

Question: *Can you wear hearing aids when you have Meniere's disease?*

Answer: *I trialled hearing aids in the early stages of Meniere's but fluctuating hearing made it impractical.*

Question: *What are grommets?*

Answer: *Grommets are small tubes, either 'T' shaped or shaped like a grommet, made of silicone or Teflon. These can be inserted under anesthetic into the eardrum, which then lets air into the middle air, affecting pressure in the fluid compartments.*

Question: *Did you try grommets for Meniere's?*

Answer: *No. I didn't want to undergo any unnecessary medical procedures. Besides, medical opinion indicates grommets are not effective.*

Question: *How is the cochlea affected by Meniere's disease?*

Answer: *When the cochlea malfunctions in Meniere's, the symptom is an acute vertigo attack. The cochlea is the hearing sense organ of the inner ear, which is divided into three chambers: two filled with a fluid called perilymph and one chamber with a fluid called endolymph. When the reissner membrane (that separates the perilymph and endolymph fluids) ruptures, the fluids mix, and it causes a vertigo attack.*

Question: *How have you dealt with hearing the loss in your life?*

Answer: *After my hearing loss stabilized, I sought help from an audiologist and purchased two hearing aids. The Meniere affected ear required considerable volume whereas the other ear affected by otosclerosis responded well to much lower volume. I also asked my partner not to talk from the other room, which she never quite got the hang of.*

Question: *Were you worried Meniere's would go to the other ear?*

Answer: *Yes, of course. There is nothing you can do but wait and see. It wasn't until the usual time limit of five years had passed, when bilateral Meniere's is most likely to happen, that I stopped worrying about bilateral Meniere's.*

Question: *What was the saddest aspect of losing hearing?*

Answer: *Knowing that it would never be found.*

Question: *What part do eyes play in Meniere's disease?*

Answer: *Meniere's affects eye movement (nystagmus), but this can vary considerably.*

Question: *What is nystagmus?*

Answer: *Nystagmus, is uncontrolled eye movement. During an attack, mixed signals are sent to the brain, which results in side to side, eye flicking (Nystagmus).*

Question: *Does Meniere's disease affect vision?*

Answer: *No, it doesn't affect or damage your vision, but I advocate regular eye checks and suitable prescription glasses (if necessary) because eyestrain can cause fatigue/stress, which can be a trigger for vertigo attacks.*

ON THE QUESTION OF FAMILY

Question: *Why is Meniere's called an invisible disease?*

Answer: *Meniere's disease is one of those invisible diseases because you can look normal and don't look ill unless you are heading for a vertigo attack, or you have just had one.*

Question: *Does Meniere's impact on close relationships?*

Answer: *Meniere's disease can dominate family life. Love in a time of Meniere's will test relationship bonds. Patience, understanding, and empathy on both sides help to reduce stress and tension. The well partner can feel quite alone when the one they love has acute attacks. As normal patterns of your old life alter, both of you must deal with the effects of chronic illness.*

Question: *What valuable advice would you give to a person who is a caregiver?*

Answer: *The partner needs to take personal time for themselves to balance their role as the caregiver. They can live in a state of anxiety, especially as they are responsible for helping and running the home. It can be a lonely time for the caregiver. Unfortunately, those most affected by the patient's illness do not always receive the support and help they need at this time. It can also be a thankless task.*

Question: *Why is it important to let the family know how you are feeling?*

Answer: *Since the acute symptoms of Meniere's disease are ongoing and episodic, it is essential to explain to your family what is happens to you. They can't mind read. It's up to you to let them know.*

ON THE QUESTION OF FRIENDS

Question: How important were friends?

Answer: Occasional contact with friends stops isolation and helps with social normality.

Question: How can friends understand Meniere's disease?

Answer: They need you to tell them what you are going through and how things are for you. Good friends are ones who stay in touch. True friends don't forget friends.

Question: How can friends help with Meniere's?

Answer: Friends can include you in activities and accept that Meniere's can make you somewhat unreliable because you might be fine on the days when you accept an invitation, but then cancel out at the last minute. Friends need to make allowances, and stay flexible, be understanding and not take last minute cancellations personally. But they need to keep including you in social activities. If they don't, it is easy for you to become isolated.

Question: *Did you tell your friends you had Meniere's?*

Answer: *Eventually, I told my close friends, mainly because they knew something was up with me. Still, not everyone knew I was ill. I am a private person and didn't disclose Meniere's to everyone. With hearing loss, I experienced a noticeable change in my ability and desire to socialize, especially in large groups.*

Question: *Were social situations a challenge?*

Answer: *The most challenging was communicating with groups of people. As my hearing deteriorated, I misheard a lot, and the hearing impediment made it difficult to have an easy conversation. I am a reasonably intelligent man who likes to have a chat, but mishearing words, and misinterpreting what people say, was a real disadvantage. At times I would miss the gist of what was said. This led to people leaving me out of the conversation.*

Question: *When you were at a social gathering, what did you do if you were feeling bad?*

Answer: *I would just slip away quietly.*

Question: *How did late nights affect you?*

Answer: *Often, a late-night would precede a vertigo attack. Late nights were something I avoided. I did everything not to get overtired. It took me a few years to stay up late enough to see a New Year in.*

ON THE QUESTION OF MENIERE'S DISEASE

Question: *How long since you recovered from Meniere's?*

Answer: *I recovered eighteen years ago, but you never forget the experience. The impact is life long.*

Question: *How do you pronounce Meniere's?*

Answer: *\men-'yerz-*

Question: *Is Meniere's disease hereditary?*

Answer: *While Meniere's disease is not genetic or hereditary, the incidence is slightly higher in some families. But no one knows the reason. Meniere's is said to be familial, with 7% to 10% of people diagnosed.*

Question: *Who first discovered Meniere's disease?*

Answer: *Prosper Meniere, a French physician, was born in Angers France, in 1799. He was the first to identify a medical condition combining vertigo, hearing loss, and tinnitus, which is now known as Meniere's disease. He finished his medical studies in Paris in 1826 and was hired as a physician-in-chief at the Institute for the Deaf and Mute. While working there, he became interested in diseases of the ear.*

Question: *What year was Meniere's disease accepted?*

Answer: *Prosper Meniere formulated a paper on a particular kind of hearing loss and episodic vertigo resulting from lesions of the inner ear in 1861. However, Meniere's disease wasn't accepted until the late 19th century. Over 150 years later, the medical profession is still trying to find the cause and cure for Meniere's disease. To date, Meniere's has proven to be an elusive condition to cure.*

Question: *How is Meniere disease spelled?*

Answer: *Two ways. Prosper Meniere was known to write his name as Menière, while his son used the spelling Ménière. Many people omit the accent marks when writing the word.*

Question: *What is the definition of Meniere's disease?*

Answer: *Meniere's, by definition, is a disorder or disease of the inner ear labyrinth, marked by unprovoked, recurring, and sudden episodes of disabling vertigo. These episodes are known as attacks that have a fluctuating hearing loss (in* *the low frequencies), and a sensation of rotational spinning (vertigo), which gives a false sense of movement. During an attack, there is nausea, vomiting, sweating, tinnitus. Recurring attacks lead to a permanent hearing loss in the affected ear and chronic tinnitus.*

Question: *What is Meniere's disease, also known as?*

Answer: *Meniere's disease is also known as idiopathic endolymphatic hydrops: Idiopathic referring to a condition of increased hydraulic pressure within the inner ear.*

Question: *Is Meniere's disease contagious?*

Answer: *Meniere's disease is not contagious. You can't catch Meniere's like a cold or flu. You can't give Meniere's to another person by contact, using the same utensils or breathing or coughing on them. In a household where one person has Meniere's, there is no chance other family members will be infected or come down with Meniere's; it's not infectious.*

Question: *Name five famous people who had Meniere's?*

Answer: *Famous people who had (or are believed to have had) Meniere's include: Alan Shepard, Vincent Van Gogh, Jonathan Swift, Marilyn Munroe, Marnie Eisenhower, Goya, Charles Darwin, Peggy Lee, Martin Luther, Emily Dickenson. The list goes on through centuries. In the world today, there are millions of people living with and coping with Meniere's disease.*

Question: *How common is Meniere's disease?*

Answer: *It is estimated there are 165,000 existing sufferers and 45,000 new cases diagnosed every year in the United States. In the UK, it's estimated that 157 per 100,000 people have Meniere's disease.*

Question: *What is the typical age range to be diagnosed with Meniere's disease?*

Answer: *The peak age for Meniere's disease is in the 40-60 year age group.*

Question: *Were you in this age group?*

Answer: *Yes, I was forty-six years old when diagnosed.*

Question: *Do both young and older people get Meniere's?*

Answer: *Yes. Meniere's disease can affect all ages. It appears in children as young as four and people over the age of ninety. However, the most common age range is from forty-nine to sixty-seven years of age.*

Question: *Is Meniere's more common in Men? Or woman?*

Answer: *Both sexes are equally affected, although some recent studies show Meniere's disease is slightly more common in women than men.*

Question: *Do you have Meniere's in your family?*

Answer: *No, not in recent family history, as far as I know.*

Question: *Are you worried you may have passed on Meniere's disease to your children?*

Answer: *No. However, one of my adult children, who was witness to my struggle with Meniere's, is now cautious about the possibility of a genetic propensity for Meniere's. She decided to work four days a week, to balance her business and private life. My eldest child, who was older at the time of my diagnosis and away at university, is the complete opposite, and a workaholic. I have cautioned him about the issues of stress over forty.*

Question: *Did Beethoven have Meniere's disease?*

Answer: *Beethoven probably suffered from both Meniere's disease and lead poisoning. He endured hearing loss and eventually went completely deaf. He also suffered severe tinnitus. Beethoven often complained: 'My ears whistle and buzz all day and all night. I can say I am living a wretched life.'*

Question: *Can migraines cause Meniere's disease?*

Answer: *There is a growing body of evidence that Meniere disease and migraine headaches may be related and/or a different spectrum of the same disease. But, there is no conclusive research that migraines cause Meniere's disease.*

Question: *Does loud music cause Meniere's disease?*

Answer: *Exposure to loud music can cause or aggravate tinnitus (ringing in the ears) and cause temporary or permanent hearing loss. However, while loud music causes trauma to the sensitive hearing mechanisms and consequent damage to the ear, there is no conclusive evidence that loud noise is an actual cause of Meniere's disease.*

Question: *Can a fall cause Meniere's disease?*

Answer: *The causes of Meniere's disease is unknown, but in my personal experience, I suffered a trauma to the side of my head, which is the same side I later experienced Meniere's.*

Question: *Can a head injury cause Meniere's?*

Answer: *Millions of dollars and years of research have been investigating the causes: one of which is the possibility arising from physical trauma, as in head injuries.*

Question: *Can the herpes virus cause Meniere disease?*

Answer: *Some studies found a possible connection to the herpes simplex virus (HSV) but do not conclude that HSV causes Meniere's disease.*

Question: *Is there a connection between the temporomandibular joint (TMJ) and Meniere's disease?*

Answer: *There are reported cases of Meniere's syndrome being relieved through neuromuscular treatment, which aligned the jaw properly. This, in turn, relieves stress on the socket of the TM Joint and allows the balance organs, which are incredibly close to the socket, to go back to normal.*

Question: *Is Meniere's disease an autoimmune disease?*

Answer: *The immune response research for Meniere's disease focuses on inner ear antigens. Approximately one-third of Meniere's disease cases seem to be of an autoimmune origin, although it's not fully understood why this is the case.*

Question: *Did Van Gogh, the Impressionist artist, have Meniere's disease?*

Answer: *Art-loving audiologists debate whether it was Meniere's that drove the artist to cut off his ear, or did the artist Gauguin cut of Van Gogh's earlobe during a fight in a bordello? No one will know for sure, as accounts on events differ. But from all historical records, the famous Impressionist artist had a hearing impairment, vertigo and tinnitus. In his letters, he describes classic Meniere symptoms; ringing and roaring in his ears, intolerance for loud noises, and dizziness.*

Question: *Does Meniere's disease cause blackouts?*

Answer: *No, Meniere's doesn't cause blackouts.*

Question: *Can Meniere's disease cause a loss of consciousness when you're having an attack?*

Answer: *No, The only time Meniere's would cause loss of consciousness is, if you fell and knocked yourself out.*

Question: *Can Meniere's disease cause a stiff neck?*

Answer: *No, Meniere's doesn't cause a stiff neck. However, periods of acute vertigo with nystagmus, plus the head tension of constant balance correction, can often manifest in a stiff neck.*

Question: *Does Meniere's disease cause itchy ears?*

Answer: *No. It causes aural fullness.*

Question: *Does Meniere's disease cause jaw pain?*

Answer: *No. Meniere's does not cause jaw pain.*

Question: *Does Meniere's disease cause joint pain?*

Answer: *No. Meniere's doesn't cause joint pain.*

Question: *Can Meniere's disease cause abdominal pain?*

Answer: *Meniere's is known to cause diarrhea and associated abdominal irritation during a vertigo attack.*

Question: *Does Meniere's disease cause excessive sweating?*

Answer: *Cold sweats are the result of vertigo. In the middle of an attack, you can break out in a cold sweat. Tension over threatening Meniere situations, such as constant loud noise or visual disturbances, can cause one to sweat.*

Question: *Does blood pressure affect Meniere's disease?*

Answer: *Blood pressure can increase during a vertigo attack, but blood pressure doesn't affect Meniere's disease.*

Question: *Did Meniere's give you high blood pressure?*

Answer: *No, not at all.*

Question: *Can Meniere's cause heart palpitations?*

Answer: *Meniere's vertigo attack brings fear, stress, and anxiety in its wake. Depending on how your body's fight-flight reflex kicks in, heart palpitations are possible.*

Question: *Can Meniere's affect sleep?*

Answer: *Yes. When you're under tension and stress from Meniere's, you are likely to wake more often during the night.*

ON THE QUESTION OF DIAGNOSIS

Question: *Who diagnoses Meniere's disease?*

Answer: *You can't self-diagnose Meniere's disease. Only a registered medical professional, a General Practitioner, ENT Specialist, or Meniere's disease specialist can prescribe a series of tests to conclude a diagnosis of Meniere's disease.*

Question: *Is Meniere's disease easy to diagnose?*

Answer: *Yes, a diagnosis of Meniere's disease requires two episodes of vertigo, each lasting 20 minutes or longer (but not longer than 24 hours) and a specific range of hearing loss, verified by a hearing test.*

Question: *How is Meniere's diagnosed? What medical workup does a doctor do for diagnosis?*

Answer: *The doctor will ask you to describe your symptoms and what happens during an attack. The doctor will order tests: blood tests, hearing tests, an MRI or CT scan, other tests to check your balance and neurological tests to rule out any brain issues.*

Question: *Does Meniere's show on an MRI?*

Answer: *Meniere's doesn't show on an MRI, but other diseases that have similar symptoms; such as a vestibular migraine, viral labyrinthitis, or a brain-stem stroke, will show up. The gadolinium-enhanced MRI checks the interior auditory canals, and this helps to rule out other causes.*

Question: *Can you see Meniere's disease on an MRI scan?*

Answer: *The MRI scan uses a strong magnetic field, not x-rays. MRI scans will not confirm a diagnosis of Meniere's disease. The MRI scan is a diagnosis of exclusion. It shows the internal auditory canal and excludes brain tumors.*

Question: *Is there a test for Meniere's disease?*

Answer: *There is no definitive test for Meniere's disease. However, there are two tests specific for Meniere's disease: the glycerol dehydration test, which involves ingesting a dehydrating agent called glycerol, and observing two things: a change in symptoms, and a measurable improvement in hearing. The second specific test is electrocochleography (ECoG). In this test, a sound is presented to the patient, and electrical* *information from the inner ear is then recorded and compared. There is a shaped electrical response in normal patients, but in patients with Meniere's disease, this response is significantly different.*

Question: *Is there a blood test for Meniere's disease?*

Answer: *There is no specific blood test that indicates Meniere's disease. A blood test workup when you present with Meniere's symptoms can help eliminate other possible issues, such as infection present in the body.*

Question: *Why are so many different tests used in the diagnosis of Meniere's?*

Answer: *Meniere's is not defined by its symptoms, as many disorders have the same symptoms as Meniere's disease. A series of diagnostic tests are needed to eliminate other diseases. Migraines and ear infections, which are also known to affect balance, and hearing can have the same disturbing symptoms.*

Question: *How is the correct diagnosis made?*

Answer: *A qualified medical professional makes a diagnosis by excluding other diseases with similar symptoms. If a cause for symptoms is found, then, by definition, the diagnosis will not be Meniere's disease, but some other condition. If you have the same Meniere symptoms, but no cause, then the diagnosis is Meniere's disease.*

Question: *How is an audiogram used in Meniere diagnosis?*

Answer: *Meniere's is diagnosed by hearing tests called an audiogram. An audiogram by a technician is a non-invasive, and painless. An audiometer delivers specific sounds frequencies (pure tones) at different intensities to find out how loud a sound must be, to be perceived. The results are compared to the normal hearing on each frequency on a computer graph. In Meniere's, the results show a low-frequency sensorineural hearing loss in the affected ear.*

Question: *What are the Weber test and the Rinne tests?*

Answer: *These non-invasive, painless tests use a metal tuning fork to differentiate conductive from sensorineural hearing loss. Hearing loss in Meniere's disease is a sensorineural hearing loss. Sensorineural hearing loss (SNHL) is a type of hearing loss or deafness in the inner ear.*

Question: *What happens in a Rinne test?*

Answer: *This is a test of hearing by bone and air conduction. The stem of a vibrating tuning fork is held against the bone behind the ear (bone conduction of sound); as soon as the sound is no longer perceived, the tuning fork is taken away and held close to the ear (air conduction). In normal hearing, the fork can still be heard, which indicates that the air conduction is better than bone conduction. With conductive hearing loss, bone* conduction is louder than air conduction. With sensorineural hearing loss, both air and bone conduction are reduced, but air conduction is louder at testing.

Question: *What happens in the Weber test?*

Answer: *It tests unilateral sensorineural hearing loss. A tuning fork is placed on the mid-line of the head, and you indicate in which ear the tone is louder. In the unilateral sensorineural hearing loss, the tone is louder in the normal ear because the tuning fork stimulates both inner ears equally.*

Question: *What is speech audiometry?*

Answer: *A test on speech recognition. You are given a list of words; each word has two equally accentuated syllables such as, staircase, baseball, bookshelf. You listen to these words spoken at different loudness, and you repeat them. The Audiologist notes the intensity at which you repeat fifty-percent of the words.*

Question: *Are there other hearing tests?*

Answer: *Yes. Word recognition score tests using one-syllable words to test the ability to discriminate speech sounds; tympanometry which measures the impedance of the middle ear to acoustic energy. This acoustic reflex helps eliminate the possibility of a tumor on the auditory nerve.*

Question: *Were any of the hearing tests painful?*

Answer: *No, they were all easy, non-invasive, and painless.*

Question: *Did you go to a hospital for the tests?*

Answer: *No. The specialist gave me a referral to an Audiologist. I went to her office and underwent thorough tests.*

Question: *What was the strangest test you had?*

Answer: *I had a non-invasive test called an auditory brain stem response. I sat with a latex cap on my head, rather like ones used to monitor sleep apnea, and told to relax, while the technician attached numerous surface electrodes with colored wires —these monitored brainwave responses to acoustic stimulation. The resulting brainwave patterns were fed into a computer to rule out a tumor on the brain stem. Luckily I didn't have one.*

Question: *Can you have a mild form of Meniere's disease?*

Answer: *Meniere's disease symptoms vary from person to person. No one patient has the same experiences, although the symptoms are the same. Some people I spoke with had a mild onset of symptoms they hardly noticed. Other people, like myself, experienced rapid onset, and violent symptoms. Meniere's disease can progress slowly or rapidly, and the symptoms can vary from mild to severe. Some days are severe, and other days are mild.*

Question: *Can Meniere's be misdiagnosed?*

Answer: *Quite possibly. There are diseases, known and unknown, that have the same symptoms as Meniere's disease. Patients could be misdiagnosed with Meniere's and treated for Meniere's. That is why it is essential to get a specialist's opinion.*

ON THE QUESTION OF DISABILITY

Question: *Is Meniere's disease a disability?*

Answer: *I think it is. Meniere's disease has both extensive physical and psychological issues.*

Question: *Does Meniere's qualify for disability benefits?*

Answer: *At the time of writing, if you are disabled because of Meniere's disease and the condition is so severe it keeps you from working, you may be entitled to Social Security Disability benefits. In the US, Meniere's is on the list of medical conditions for immediate approval, providing all the testing* they require has been done. In the UK, you may be able to apply for a grant for practical support to help you do your job. For those people affected by severe and frequent attacks, full time or even part-time work may not be possible, so that you may be looking to the government for benefits and allowances. Depending on your symptoms, you may be entitled to a Disability Living Allowance.

Question: Is there help with railway fares?

Answer: Yes, in the UK if you have a hearing impairment or wear a hearing aid, or, if you are on a disability benefit for Meniere's, you can apply for a Disabled Person's Railcard to receive a third off rail travel, underground rail, and some designated ferries.

Question: What're the rules about driving with Meniere's?

Answer: With any balance disorder, you must let the Department of Vehicle Licensing know. There are rules about Vertigo Vs. Driving. The DVLA may temporarily revoke a driving license due to certain medical conditions. The law on driving may be different in other countries, but to make sure you are insured to drive with Meniere's. It pays to check the law and the fine print.

Question: *What is a Blue Badge or Disabled Badge?s*

Answer: *The Blue Badge and Disabled Badge are an entitlement to disabled parking. They are not limited only to drivers; they're given to an individual who may be the passenger or the designated driver.*

Question: *Did you wear a Meniere's medical bracelet?*

Answer: *No I didn't. An identity bracelet for me would be a constant reminder of an illness. I couldn't see the need for it because you don't go unconscious during an attack! For some people, this might make them feel more secure. I don't support Meniere's merchandising; key rings, coffee mugs, or wearing, 'I have Meniere's, sweatshirts'.*

Question: *How can people get Meniere's disease support?*

Answer: *Support comes from Meniere societies, Meniere forums, Meniere support groups, Meniere blog posts, and reading as many books as you can find on the subject!*

BOOKS MENIERE MAN RECOMMENDS

Mindful Way Through Depression.

-By Jon Kabat-Zinn

Full Catastrophe Living.

-By Jon Kabat-Zinn

Mindfulness Based Stress Reduction Workbook.

-By Jon Kabat-Zinn

The Man Who Mistook His Wife for a Hat.

-By Oliver Sacks

Stumbling on Happiness.

-By Daniel Todd Gilbert

Still Alice

-By Lisa Genova

ABOUT MENIERE MAN

    With a smile and a sense of humor, the Author pens himself as Meniere Man, because, as he says, Meniere's disease changed his life dramatically. At the height of his business career and aged just 46, he suddenly became acutely ill. He was diagnosed with Meniere's disease. He began to lose all hope that he would fully recover his health. However, the full impact of having Meniere's disease was to come later. He lost not only his health but also his career and financial stability at the time.

It was his spirit and desire to get 'back to normal' that turned his life around for the better. He decided that you can't put a limit on anything in life. Rather than letting Meniere's disease get in the way of life, he started to focus on how to overcoming Meniere's disease.

With the advice on healing and recovery in his books, anyone reading the advice, can make simple changes and find a way toward a recovery from Meniere's disease. These days life is different for the Author. He is a fit man who has no symptoms of Meniere's except for tinnitus and hearing loss. He does not take any medication. All the physical activities he does these days require a high degree of balance: snowboarding, surfing, hiking, windsurfing and weight training. All these things, he started to do while suffering from Meniere's disease symptoms. Meniere Man believes that if you want to experience a marked improvement in health, you can't wait until you feel well to start. You must begin to improve your health immediately, even though you may not feel like it.

The Author is a writer, painter and designer. He is married to a Poet. They have two adult children. He spends his time writing and painting. He loves the sea, nature, cooking, travel, the company of family, friends and his beloved dog Bella.

If you enjoyed this book and you think it may be helpful to others, please leave a review for this book.

BELLA

The Meniere Man Mindful Recovery Series

The books tell how it is possible to go from a Meniere suffer to Meniere survivor. The purpose of this Mindful Recovery Series is a simple one. Each book shares Meniere Man's management methods for coping and making a full recovery from Meniere's disease.

MENIERE'S #1 BEST SELLER 3RD EDITION

MENIERE MAN
MAKE A FULL RECOVERY

**Let's
Get Better**
MY MENIERE SURVIVOR'S BOOK

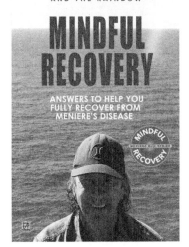

MENIERE MAN
AND THE RAINBOW

MINDFUL
RECOVERY
ANSWERS TO HELP YOU
FULLY RECOVER FROM
MENIERE'S DISEASE

MENIERE MAN
AND THE ASTRONAUT

THE
SELF HELP
BOOK FOR
MENIERE'S
DISEASE

**It's the only positive, yet real account
I've read, of what it's really like.**
- L. Forrester.(UK)

PAGE ADDIE PRESS. UNITED KINGDOM. AUSTRALIA

MENIERE MAN
AND THE FILM DIRECTOR

THE
SELF HELP
BOOK FOR
MENIERE'S
VERTIGO

*This book really helped me get up
and get moving. It helped give me the
desire to get on with life.*
- CDW

PAGE ADDIE PRESS
UNITED KINGDOM. AUSTRALIA

MENIERE MAN
AND THE BUTTERFLY

The Meniere Effect

HOW TO MANAGE
THE LIFE CHANGING
EFFECTS OF
MENIERE'S

KEEPING LIFE POSITIVE THROUGH
THE DIFFICULT TIMES OF MENIERE'S

PAGE ADDIE PRESS. UNITED KINGDOM. AUSTRALIA

MENIERE MAN
IN THE KITCHEN

RECIPES
THAT
HELPED ME
GET OVER
MENIERE'S
DISEASE

Delicious nutritious low salt
recipes from our family kitchen

PAGE ADDIE PRESS. UNITED KINGDOM. AUSTRALIA

MENIERE MAN
IN THE KITCHEN

BOOK 2
RECIPES
THAT
HELPED ME
GET OVER
MENIERE'S

DELICIOUS LOW SALT RECIPES
FROM OUR FAMILY KITCHEN

PAGE ADDIE PRESS, UNITED KINGDOM, AUSTRALIA

MENIERE MAN
IN THE KITCHEN

COOKING
FOR
MENIERE'S
THE
LOW SALT
WAY

ITALIAN

OUR MUCH LOVED ITALIAN
LOW SALT FAMILY RECIPES

PAGE ADDIE PRESS, UNITED KINGDOM, AUSTRALIA

REFERENCES

American Academy of Otolaryngology-Head and Neck Surgery's 1995

Guidelines for the Diagnosis and Evaluation of Therapy in Meniere's disease.

AAO- HNS: American Academy of Otolaryngology and Head and Neck Surgery; PTA: Pure Tone Audiometry; DHI: Dizziness Handicap Inventory

American Academy of Otolaryngology-Head and Neck Foundation, Inc.(1995). 'Committee on Hearing and Equilibrium guidelines for the diagnosis and evaluation of therapy in Meniere's disease. ' Otolaryngol Head Neck Surg 113(3): 181-185.

Anderson JP, Harris JP. Impact of Meniere's disease on quality of life. Otol Neurotol 22:888-894,2001

HAVIA M, Kentala E. Progression of symptoms of dizziness in Meniere's disease. Arch Otolaryngol Head Neck Surg 2004;130:431-5.

Honrubia V. Pathophysiology of Meniere's disease. Meniere's Disease (Ed. Harris JP) 231-260, 1999, Pub: Kugler (The Hague)

Huppert, D., et al. (2010). 'Long-term course of Meniere's disease revisited.' Acta Otolaryngol 130(6): 644-651.

MATEIJSEN DJ, Van Hengel PW, Van Huffelen WM, Wit HP, Albers FW. Pure-tone and speech audiometry in patients with Meniere's disease. Clin Otolaryngol 2001; 26: 379-87.

Santos, P. M., R. A. Hall, et al. (1993). 'Diuretic and

diet effect on Meniere's disease evaluated by the 1985 Committee on Hearing and Equilibrium guidelines.' Otolaryngol Head Neck Surg 109(4): 680-9.

Savastino M, Marioni G, Aita M. Psychological characteristics of patients with Meniere's disease compared with patients with vertigo, tinnitus or hearing loss. ENT journal, 148-156, 2007

Savastano M, Maron MB, Mangialaio M, Longhi P, Rizzardo R. Illness behavior, personality traits, anxiety and depression in patients with Meniere's disease. J Otolaryngol 1996 Oct;25(5):329-333.

Sato GI, Sekine K, Matsuda K, Ueeda H, Horii A, Nishiike S, Kitahara T, Uno A, Imai T, Inohara H, Takeda N. Long-term prognosis of hearing loss in patients with unilateral Ménière's disease. Acta Otolaryngol. 2014 Jul 16:1-6. [Epub]

Soto-Varela AI, Huertas-Pardo B, Gayoso-Diz P, Santos-Perez S, Sanchez-Sellero I. Disability perception in Ménière's disease: when, how much and why? Eur Arch Otorhinolaryngol. 2015 May 1. [Epub]

Stahle J, Friberg U, Svedberg A. Long-term progression of Meniere's disease. Acta Otolaryngol (Stockh) 1991:Suppl 485:75-83

Thirlwall, A. S. and S. Kundu (2006). 'Diuretics for Meniere's disease or syndrome.' Cochrane Database Syst Rev 3: CD003599.

'Ménière's Disease.' The Alternate Advisor: The Complete Guide to Natural Therapies and Alternative Treatments. Edited by Robert. Richmond, VA: Time-Life Books, 1997

MENIERE SUPPORT

Meniere's Society (UNITED KINGDOM)
www. menieres.org.uk
Meniere's Society Australia (AUSTRALIA)
info@menieres.org.au
The Meniere's Resource & Information Centre (AUSTRALIA)
www.menieres.org.au
Healthy Hearing & Balance Care (AUSTRALIA)
www.healthyhearing.com.au
Vestibular Disorders association (AUSTRALIA)
www.vestibular .org
The Dizziness and Balance Disorders Centre (Australia)
www.dizzinessbalancedisorders.com
Meniere's Research Fund Inc   (AUSTRALIA)
www.menieresresearch.org.au
Australian Psychological Society APS (AUSTRALIA)
www.psychology.org.au
Meniere's Disease Information Center (USA)
www.menieresinfo.com
Vestibular Disorders Association (USA)
www.vestibular.org
BC Balance and Dizziness Disorders Society (CANADA)
www.balanceand dizziness.org
Hearwell (NEW ZEALAND)
www.hearwell.co.nz
WebMD.
www.webmd.com
National Institute for Health
www.medlineplus.gov
Mindful Living Program
www.mindfullivingprograms.com
Center for Mindfulness
www. umassmed.edu.com

Notes